Be The Police Supervisor

Preparing For The Test And The Job

John L. Gray, M.Ed.
Police Chief and Test Developer

with

Laurie L. Gray, B.S.
Educator and Test Administrator

John L. Gray and Laurie L. Gray

Retails sales of this book can be found at Amazon.com
Inquiries for bulk sales at a substantial discount can be directed to the JL Gray Company

Published by the JL Gray Company, Everett, Washington
www.jlgraycompany.com
Email: johnlgray425@icloud.com

TABLE OF CONTENTS

ACKNOWLEDGMENTS

You would not be reading this unless you were really serious about doing well on the promotional test and laying the foundation to do the job. The fact that you are serious has already separated you from most of the competing candidates.

A work like this is the summation of a huge collection of wisdom from many successful leaders. I have been blessed with 32 years of experience with 14 years supervision and management that include 12 years as a Police Chief. Along the way, I accumulated a wealth of knowledge from great classes, training sessions, and conferences. Then, I rubbed shoulders with some of the best leaders in public service who shared their wisdom and lessons learned. My intention is to couple that knowledge and experience with 8 years of working full-time, creating and administering over 150 processes with 400 assessors and 800 candidates, to create a product that is really useful for you.

Our company is dedicated to developing the next leaders in public safety. This book and that work would not be possible without today's leaders who shared their knowledge and lessons and who want to continue to improve the profession and better serve their communities.

This goal would never be met without you, the candidate, who demonstrates the courage to step out of your comfort zone of being the master level employee and strives to join the small group of leaders who lead the employees at our police agencies.

Thank you, because the future of our profession is in your hands.

Introduction

This book started out as an update to our book <u>Going The Distance, A Candidate's Guide to Promotional Testing and Assessment Centers</u> because we wanted to add much more detail after four years in print. Instead, it turned into a complete re-write with the focus on what the title says: **Be The Police Supervisor.** This work is intended to be a reference to assist you in preparing for the next job promotion. This book is grounded from our experience from the public sector and specifically with law enforcement agencies.

This book is also intended to be a stand-alone resource as you prepare for the promotional test. Though we have created and administered over 150 promotional processes and trained test developers, we have tried to make the information useful and applicable to other testing models. It is impossible to create a useful book that can apply to every test provider's process. The staff person or test provider that plans and conducts your agency's promotional process may have unique pieces that may or may not agree with this material. But we hope the topics presented here will be helpful for you and at the minimum, will inspire you to ask the test provider informed questions that are suggested here.

Much of the content of this book is focused on the first level supervisor because the first promotion into a leadership position is the hardest to attain. Only 4% of the workforce is in positions of supervision or management. You are working to join an elite group that is hard to join because the transition from line employee to supervisor is the hardest to make because it requires a shift in your thinking. You were carefully selected and trained for the position that you have and your organization, the supervisors and the trainers reinforce the way to think and the best way to do your job every day. Now, you will need to shift your thinking to what a supervisor does, how they do their job and why they make the choices that they do.

One of our goals with this book is that you will **not** make the most common mistake at your promotional test: to think and act like you are testing for the job that you already have. That is why master officers, master deputies, master detectives, candidates with many years of experience or have advanced college degrees who take the promotional test repeatedly will not be selected. They look good on paper but do not think like a supervisor.

The promotional testing process is more about assessing your change of thinking to be a supervisor and that is why all the good work that you have done is not an assurance that you will be promoted. And, that is why officers who were only above average performers get promoted – they have made that thinking shift. That change in thinking and how to do it is a central theme in this book.

The other reason we have focused on testing for a position as a supervisor is that there are more candidates and more testing for this position than any other. However, we have also included themes and examples for command level management positions as well.

Frankly, this book is more than what the title says; it is also a glimpse of what great supervisors and managers are, what they do and why they do it that way. We have woven into the chapters many lessons and advice about good supervision, management and leadership that was taken from expectations written for agencies and from training courses. The intention of this book is to help guide you in your professional development, because great people who take ownership of their career and are intentional in their learning will become the leaders of great agencies.

As a Police Chief who advanced through the ranks, I have taken a variety of promotional processes, succeeded at most and did poorly on some. As a manager, I participated in creating the promotional processes for my agency and served as an assessor for many agencies. As an instructor, I taught this topic at a national command school. Since retiring from full-time police work and over an eight-year period, we have created and administered over 150 processes, involving over 800 candidates for positions that ranged from first level supervisor to chief executive and everything in-between.

This book is intended to help take away some of the mystery of the testing process and to roll up the curtain behind promotional testing because this may reduce your anxiety and allow you to excel. Preventable anxiety and fear are the most common barriers to being successful. We want great candidates to succeed at the promotional process because you are the future of the profession.

The design of this book includes separating out key themes to help you in your learning. We have bolded words and phrases to get your attention. At the end of each chapter, the key themes are listed. Here is the first key theme:

Key Theme: Being you is an important part of the path to being a top tier candidate. Be authentic, genuine and show your true character. Do not be an actor, a pretender, or attempt to deceive the assessors, as this is the surest way to fail.

This book is intended to be one of the elements of a strategy of preparation because the **most prepared candidate** often finishes in the top tier. The other parts of your preparation strategy should include:

- ✓ Do the best day-to-day performance possible,
- ✓ Follow the examples of excellent supervisors,
- ✓ Seek out opportunities to lead,
- ✓ Learn from mistakes and the lessons of others,
- ✓ Be the model of the attitude that you want to see in others,
- ✓ Be the best example of your agency's mission and values, and
- ✓ Develop and continue to hone a full and mature set of technical skills.

Details on these and other ways to prepare are the central topics of this book.

For many police agencies, the gold standard of promotional testing is the assessment center process for reasons that will be explained later. There are other promotional processes that are chosen because they are easier to create and administer or are less expensive. Except for the first chapter, this work will focus on the assessment center process. However, nearly all of this material can be effectively applied to other testing processes as well, because the assessment center process is the most complex testing process and the most challenging for the candidate. When you study and prepare for the most challenging task, the simpler ones will be easier.

No introduction on how to prepare would be complete without a cautionary note. There is a lot of information out there on how to do well on a promotional test. Be careful what you study and be a bit skeptical of suggestions that are advertised as being "the best answer." The best answer is a blend that demonstrates your knowledge, skills and abilities, your knowledge of your agency's policies and procedures, embraces your agency's vision, mission and values, and shows your character, maturity, wisdom and enthusiasm for the job.

Key Theme: The best answer in a promotional process comes from your personal development and experience that is rooted in being well rounded, fully developed and a person of character and maturity.

Always be honest and in-the-moment with the assessors. Do not recite rote-memorized answers that are not yours. Candidates who deliver what they think the assessors want to hear rarely reach the top tier because part of the assessment is to reveal the candidate's character, maturity and wisdom.

We often saw candidates who just want to experience the testing process and do not really want to be a supervisor. They often did this by viewing the process as just a learning opportunity. Perhaps, if they would read and study this material, they would achieve their goal. These testing processes are expensive in terms of money, effort and time, and there is often a limitation on the number of candidates who can participate. Having candidates who are not fully committed may deny a testing opportunity to someone who seriously wants to be a supervisor.

We have seen candidates who have approached the preparation for the promotional process as an "event" rather than an **example of their lifestyle** and the test day is simply a stage to perform on. Candidates who do this often receive marginal scores, because the seasoned assessors will detect the shallowness and narrowness of the candidate's knowledge, skills, abilities and attitude, if not the deceptive behavior.

Preparing for the promotion process starts the day you decide to commit to the journey of self-improvement and continues through your whole career. Marginal candidates view preparation as a sprint that started when the announcement of the test was posted. Top candidates begin their preparation much, much earlier and view it as a lifestyle. They are the ones who will succeed by thinking and acting like a supervisor.

THE KEY THEMES IN REVIEW:

- ✓ Being you is an important part of the path to being a top tier candidate. Be authentic, genuine and show your true character. Do not be an actor, a pretender, or attempt to deceive the assessors, as this is the surest way to fail.

✓ The best answer in a promotional process comes from your personal development and experience that is rooted in being well rounded, fully developed and a person of character and maturity.

Chapter 1

The Promotional Test

Testing is a part of the process to select the next supervisor because it makes the decision more objective and guides the decision makers in choosing the most qualified candidate. Make no mistake, the promotional testing process is a competition between candidates who meet the minimum qualifications and is a weeding out process that separates the top candidates from the rest. Who gets hired and who is promoted are the most important decisions that the employer will make since these can have the most long lasting impacts on the agency and the community.

Your first goal is be successful at completing **all** of the steps of the promotional process and to NOT be weeded out. The second goal is to be in the top tier of candidates.

The intention of this chapter is to share what great testing looks like so you can be a better candidate by knowing what to expect and to understand the parts of the process. Typically, the personnel rules at your agency will spell out the requirements of the promotional test and what the components will be.

Sometimes, the requirements are included in the Collective Bargaining Agreement between the union and your employer. Also, look at your agency's policy and procedure manual. Knowing your personnel rules and the administrative guidelines, you should be able to find the answers to these questions:

✓ What are the minimum qualifications to apply? These may be expressed in years of service or education requirements.

✓ What are the components of the test? More about these are described later.

✓ Is weighting of the test components allowed? If so, what are they? For example, the written examination is worth 1/3 and the assessment center is worth 2/3 of the final score.

✓ Is there a minimum or passing score? Sometimes, the minimum passing score will be 70%. The more progressive employers often do not have a passing score for promotional tests because labeling a competent and valued employee who earned a low score as a failure can have a number of unintended consequences. The low scoring candidates are not promoted, so what is the point of the label, "failed?"

✓ What does the **Job Description** say? The valid testing process is tied to the current job description and this document will list the major tasks and functions of the position. It is these tasks and functions that a good test will measure. The test provider will be referring to the Job Description while building your test.

✓ When is the promotional test conducted? This will guide you in the timeliness and urgency of your preparation.

Key Theme: As the candidate, researching and knowing the answers to the topics and questions above and other topics will create the foundation for preparing for the selection process.

If you cannot find the answers by reading, make an appointment to ask your human resources or personnel staff these questions. Do not be fearful of this conversation because most human resources specialists will welcome the questions.

To formally start the testing process, your employer will typically create and post a **Job Announcement** that will describe the essential information about the job and the test, including the requirements, the dates and deadlines, and what the test components will be. A well-constructed test will stay within the boundaries of the Job Announcement. Study this announcement carefully and read into the meanings of the details. Do not make the mistake of preparing for topics or a process that are not described in the Job Announcement. As a candidate, the Job Announcement should answer your top tier of questions.

The ideal promotional process is **valid, objective and defensible**. Let's drill down on those three terms in a way that may be useful as you shift your thinking to be the supervisor.

Validity. There are books and courses on this subject and experts who have earned advanced degrees in this field. In the world of testing, there are two principle paths to validate a test. One is using a statistical process from surveys and test results to create a body of empirical evidence that proves the test is valid. The second path, and the most common, is called "Content

Validity." Here, a subject matter expert (also known as a SME) or a panel of experts reviews the content of the test and states the test is valid for the context it was built for. Meaning, that the test is valid for this specific agency and this specific position. Often, the subject matter expert for your agency's test will be a senior manager of your agency.

When a test is not specific to the agency, not built to the specifics of the Job Description, or not built on the foundation of the agency's policies and practices; the test could be successfully challenged for not being valid.

Common to both paths of validity is the necessity for a current Job Task Analysis (known as a JTA) because this identifies the top tier tasks that the position currently does. Typically, the employer will do the Job Task Analysis and this document helps identify the topics that should be included in the test. The current professional practice is to do a Job Task Analysis when the position's duties or responsibilities have changed.

Ask the current supervisors if they recently completed a survey about importance of the tasks that they do. If they did, it was probably a Job Task Analysis. Ask the fair question about which tasks were most important because this is another clue on how to focus your preparation.

An indicator that a test is valid is when the candidates say that the test was realistic; it felt like the job they were testing for.

Objective. This means that the test's content measures the candidate's characteristics that minimize the subjective judgments about the candidate and the person scoring it. Characteristics, in this context, typically means the candidate's possession of the body of knowledge required for the job and the skills and abilities necessary to perform the job. All of these should result in an empirical score. A better test provides evidence to support the empirical score and this evidence is often the assessor's observations. The best test has guidelines and training for the assessors on how to determine their scores. Without clear guidelines by the employer and good training on how to apply these, the well-intentioned assessor will apply their guidelines in determining their score and this will undermine the objectivity of the test.

An example of the scoring of a test that is not objective would be test scores that are only a collection of the assessor's opinions and are without scores, evidence, and guidelines or expectations.

Defensible. This means the testing process can withstand legal challenges. This also includes that the content of the test was appropriate and reasonable for the job being tested for. The foundation of this is the current **Job Description** for the position being tested for. Constructing a Job Description has a number of categories including the required knowledge, skills and abilities or KSA's. The KSA's will drive what the test will cover. The Job Description and the Job Task Analysis are typically done by the employer's personnel specialist and then approved by the employer.

Key Theme: Study the Job Description and the Job Announcement to focus on your preparation.

Be serious about committing your efforts to the testing process because your employer will most likely be spending a lot of money in time and materials for the testing process. Therefore, the promotional testing process is a big deal for both you and your employer. When you commit to matching the commitment, time, and energy in preparation that your employer is making to create the process, you will be on the right path to succeeding.

Who makes the decisions about the components and the content of the test? Typically, this is a joint venture between the agency's leadership team, the test provider, the personnel specialist and the civil service commission. We use the term civil service commission but this applies to all boards, commissions and persons of authority who provide oversight of the testing process.

Key Theme: Part of your preparation is to research the prior promotional test processes for your agency. What has been done successfully in the past is a good indicator of what may happen again.

THE TRADITIONAL PROMOTIONAL TEST PROCESS

The traditional test process that has been happening for decades is still common today. The components of the traditional promotional test are often similar to the ones for the entry-level officer test: Application, Written Test, and Interview. For agencies that have not changed in many years, the assumption is that what worked for the entry-level test will work well for the promotional test. Though that assumption is in question and progressive employers have moved away from this model, this format is very much alive and well, so let's talk about it since the ideal promotional test has these components plus more.

✓ **Application.** The application is your formal written intent that you will be participating in the promotional process. The application may be in the form of an online template, a formatted letter of interest, or a hardcopy form. Completing the application offers your proof that you meet the minimum qualifications and requirements. Occasionally, we have seen the application scored for writing skills; so make it your best work.

The KEYS TO SUCCESS are:
1. Pay attention to the instructions and the information in the Job Announcement.
2. Fully and clearly address ALL of the requirements or minimum qualifications. Sometimes potentially great and qualified candidates are eliminated in this small and initial step; do not be one of them!
3. Meet the deadlines required and complete the application well before the final hour to make certain that is received and processed on time.

✓ **Written Examination.** Before we talk about the skill of written test taking, let's talk about the marginal written examinations because there are a lot of them. The are many reasons that a written examination could be a marginal one and the most common are: old and outdated, the questions are poorly constructed, there are "trick" answers, and/or the examination is on information that is not specific to the job being tested for or does not apply to the agency.

Unfortunately, many agencies continue to use old or

outdated written examinations because the decision to use them is more about budget or meeting a deadline than the quality of the testing process. These outdated examinations were developed or purchased at a time that does not reflect what the job currently does or the agency's critical policies and procedures have changed.

We have seen many written examinations that are poorly constructed. An example of this is the test question on an agency's policy and procedure. The test question is fill-in-the-blank that requires the candidate to properly recite a set of words or phrases. These tests are easy to write but the weakness is interpreting the candidate's answer. What if the answer has most of the required words, do they get full or partial credit? If partial credit is given, what are the criteria? What if another word that has a similar meaning is used? What assurances are there that the scoring was done consistently between questions and between candidates? These questions and others like them can create a fertile ground for preventable appeals or challenges.

There are many examinations that are off-the-shelf for police sergeant and other jobs but they are not specific to the unique duties and tasks of your agency. Also, these examinations may not have the look and feel of your agency. Tests like these also have more generalized topics like reading comprehension, spelling and grammar and math problems. The topics may have been validated for the profession on a national level but may or may not be the best test available for your specific agency.

The better examinations and how to prepare for them are

covered in the Job Knowledge Test section that follows.

The KEYS TO SUCCESS for written examinations are:

1. Discover the source materials for the examination and study them.
2. If a study guide is available, get it and use it.
3. Test taking is a skill that can be learned and improved. Therefore, find practice examinations that are available online. Do not let this important opportunity be the only time that you have taken a written examination since being hired or attended school.
4. The better-written tests are only multiple choice and typically the professional test writer will distribute the correct answer among all four options. Meaning that, generally, if there are 100 questions, 25 answers will be answer A, 25 will be answer B, etc.
5. Stick to your initial gut feeling about an answer. Research shows that when answers are changed, most of the time they are changed to a wrong answer.

✓ **Interview.** The traditional interview typically draws questions from the categories of Personal Insight and Specific Issue. Rather than covering this here, see the concepts that start on page 122 that will cover these topics in depth.

✓ **Rule of 3 or 5.** These are the top number of candidates, usually 3 or 5, who are often evaluated by the leadership team for one characteristic: the best fit for the job and the organization. In most personnel rules, this top number of candidates is essentially equal and the leadership team can choose anyone. The leadership team can be subjective and are not required to explain or defend their decision.

✓ **Probation.** The period of probation is often 6 months or a year. This period allows the candidate to work in the job and demonstrate that they have the capacity to be successful in the long term. Usually, the employer does not have to explain or defend their decision to fail a candidate during the probationary period.

The Ideal Promotional Test Process

We have seen a lot of traditional and flawed promotional processes. The ideal promotional test is multi-dimensional with more components than the traditional test process, provides the candidate more opportunities to show their knowledge, skills and abilities, and involves many assessors to assess the candidate's qualifications. The additional opportunities or "looks" are:

✓ **Letter of Interest and Resume.** This is often a structured document where the candidate needs to address a number of topics such as experience, education and training. Often, there are a few questions about motivation, character, and values that need to be answered. Sometimes, these are provided to the assessors at the assessment center and the work performance assessment (more on this later) and these are scored as a part of the testing process. A well-written test announcement will describe what needs to be done and will specify if the letter of interest or resume are part of the evaluation process.

This element is very common for promotional processes for management and executive positions.

✓ **Job Knowledge Test.** This is generally a 100-question, multiple-choice test that is tailored to the agency and to the job. The information used to formulate the questions is what should supervisors have "between their ears." Meaning, in the world of easy access to policy and procedure, what should the supervisor have to immediately know? These questions typically come from critical policies and practices, governing laws and rules, the collective bargaining agreement and personnel rules, a textbook that is current and relevant, and recent and relevant court decisions.

Competent and professional human resource staff will pilot test a written examination with people currently in the position. This step will often identify problem questions and ensure that the content of the test is valid.

Good test question writers do not write trick questions, they write good distracting answers. Trick questions will: use the word "except," have answers with double negatives, the question is about minor and irrelevant information like statute numbers, and answers will be a combination of other answers like "A and B."

You will have no control over the test questions. Getting through trick questions is done by a mastery of the information. Challenging a test question is often an option. You will need to know the process and timeline of that process. We have seen the results of a written test changed by successful challenges of test questions.

✓ **Work Performance Assessment.** This is a method used by more and more agencies to assign a score to the quality of the candidate's recent job performance. Candidates are scored by the agency's supervisors on a set of performance dimensions. How scoring is done, the kinds of information to be considered and how information is shared during the scoring process are carefully done by the test provider to keep the process valid and defensible. Examples of performance dimensions for first-line supervisor are:

- o Demonstrates Responsible & Ethical Behavior
- o Demonstrates the Agency's Mission and Values
- o Demonstrates Quality of Work
- o Demonstrates Quantity of Work
- o Demonstrates Leadership

Examples of performance dimensions for command and management positions are:

- o Demonstrates Command Character
- o Demonstrates Trustworthiness
- o Demonstrates Management Skills
- o Demonstrates Command Judgment & Decisiveness
- o Demonstrates Leadership

Remember, these performance dimensions are intended to capture many skills, abilities and characteristics, to give credit for the candidate's work quality, and their contributions to the employer. This component helps the great employee who had a bad day on test day and helps eliminate the marginal employee who is a great test taker or a "one-day wonder on test day."

✓ **Job Simulations.** A job simulation or exercise is more than a hypothetical question, "What would you do if this happened?" A job simulation is actually doing the task while being watched by the assessors. A job simulation will separate out the candidates who like the idea of being a supervisor from ones who have the skills and abilities to be a leader because experiencing the stress often strips away faked responses. Experiencing a few job simulations are the foundation of an assessment center and the bulk of this book is devoted to this topic. So read on.

The following additional components to the traditional testing process may not be equally weighted and agencies approach that differently. After the top tier candidates are identified, there are often additional components that are intended to determine which of the most qualified candidates are the right fit for the current promotional opportunity and those are:

✓ **Interview.** You probably noticed that this component is placed after the written test, work performance assessment and the job simulations. Why? Interviews are inherently subjective and therefore are better used later in the process on the Rule of 3 or 5 candidates. But tradition is hard to break.

✓ **Personality Assessment Survey.** The notion behind this tool is to better know the candidate's strengths and weaknesses but in the context of helping them be more effective as an employee. There are a variety of assessment tools available and most of them are taken online. These are not scored and typically are not part of the competitive process. Employers who use these tools and the candidates who experience them, give them high marks. Typically, a report is generated for the employer that gives an indication of what the candidate's strengths and weaknesses are in the context of the work setting. Often, the candidate gets a report that is focused on how to guide self-improvement. The better instruments will include recommendations for the employer to help the candidate be more successful.

THE KEY THEMES IN REVIEW:

- ✓ Approach the test process as being successful at <u>every</u> step, even the smallest one, because candidates who do not complete a step are weeded-out.

- ✓ Discover the answers to these questions:

    - What are the minimum qualifications?

    - What are the components of the test?

    - Is weighting the test components allowed and what are they?

    - Is there a minimum passing score for each component or the whole test?

    - What was the prior testing process?

- ✓ Study the Job Description and the Job Announcement to focus on your preparation.

✓ Part of your preparation is to research the prior promotional test processes for your agency. What has been done successfully in the past is a good indicator of what may happen again.

✓ Taking a written examination is a skill that can be enhanced through study and practice. Study the topic of test taking and take sample written tests. Do not let an important promotional test that often happens ever two or three years, be the first time you have taken one.

Chapter 2

What Is An Assessment Center

Assessment centers are essentially a collection of job-related exercises or simulations where you will need to think, act and talk like you are in the position being tested for. Simply, you _are_ the supervisor or manager. Trained assessors will evaluate your performance using a set of behavioral dimensions and, in the better assessment centers, your final score comes from a multi-component empirical process rather than a consensus of opinions.

Let's break down the key parts of these concepts:

1. There is a "**collection of job-related simulations or exercises**" meaning there are at least three exercises, four is better and the most common, and five exercises are best. The notion is that the more "looks" that a candidate receives during the testing process the better. The collection of exercises should span the diversity of the position's major duties and responsibilities in order to give you the opportunity to demonstrate the depth of your professional skill set and personal characteristics. There will

be more about the kinds of exercises in Chapter Eight.

2. **"Job-related"** means the exercises will be based on some of the core or principle tasks that the position does. The core tasks are those that are that are done frequently or are very important. For example, a daily task may be sorting through messages and information and making decisions or an important task. Though not a frequent task, an important one is managing a critical field event or counseling an employee about a performance issue.

As we mentioned in the previous chapter, the exercises are validated by a Subject Matter Expert and are typically based on the core tasks that are identified in the Job Task Analysis.

From this survey or another method to determine the core tasks, the test provider and the Subject Matter Expert will build the job simulations and the other test components that relate to the top tier of job tasks.

Key Theme: Be sure you know what the position does, what the major duties are, and prepare accordingly. The **Job Description** for the position being tested will provide this information. Focus your preparation on the major duties that the position either frequently does or are very important. Marginal candidates will get bogged down in the minor tasks, the rare and exceptional task or procedural work, and miss the larger duties and responsibilities. What is the best way to find out what the important or frequent tasks are? Simply, go ask the people who are in the position.

3. The **"exercises or job-simulations"** are generally chosen by your agency. Some test providers have off-the-shelf exercises that are built and ready to use. However, these still need to be validated by the SME because the job simulations should **not**

have major themes or important information that are **not** associated with the position being tested for.

An example of a poorly designed test component that could be challenged is a job simulation where the candidate counsels an employee for a violation of a policy relating to social media. However, the agency's policy was in the process of approval and was not finalized before the test. In this case, the assessors would use the standards and expectations that they use *by their agency* to grade the candidate. In this example, the test is flawed on two levels. First, the social media policy was not approved and not distributed. Second, the assessors were not provided the agency's specific expectations of a strong candidate.

Another current professional practice is the job simulation or exercise will have the look and feel of the work being done by the current people who are in the position being tested for. This means that streets, businesses, staffing levels, available resources and terminology are realistic. This is the weakness of an off-the-shelf job simulation that has not been tailored to the agency. For example, the candidate from a medium sized suburban area is asked to address a complex event in a major city and coordinate resources that the medium sized agency does not have.

4. The "**need to think, act and talk like you are in the position**" is not about acting or pretending but about *genuinely demonstrating* your raw abilities to do the job. This can only happen when you have made the shift of thinking from being an officer to being a supervisor. The assessment center is not about responding to hypothetical events where you would be tentative in your responses; it is about acting appropriately as the actual

supervisor or manager. This is about fully engaging with the role players, viewing the exercise as the real thing and fully explaining the reasons behind your decisions and actions in the job simulations and exercises. Higher scoring candidates will demonstrate their knowledge, character, leadership attributes, and their command and communication skills during the exercise. Underlying these, the top candidates show their desire, commitment, enthusiasm and passion for this job.

Key Theme: The assessors can only score you on what you say and do. If you do not say it or do it, you cannot receive credit for it. In nearly every assessment, an assessor will say that they felt a candidate was qualified and could do the job, but the candidate did not *demonstrate* their skills or *fully explain* the reasons behind their decisions or actions and therefore received lower scores.

5. What you do and say during an exercise is "**evaluated by trained assessors.**" This means that you will encounter multiple assessors who will be scoring you. Typically, assessors are assigned to an exercise rather than to a candidate. So, if there are four exercises, you will meet four sets of assessors. A minimum of two assessors are needed for each exercise and the number can be as high as 4 assessors per exercise. The assessors will have experienced a training session on how to score, guidelines that describe what strong candidates look like and how to conduct the exercise. Chapter 5 explains this topic in greater detail.

6. Your performance is assessed using a "**set of behavioral dimensions.**" The test provider may use a different term but the concept is the same: a behavioral dimension is a set of

predetermined traits or categories of characteristics, knowledge, skills and abilities. When you do an Internet search for assessment centers, you will find a long list of different behavioral dimensions used by different test providers. However, they generally fall within the reasonable skills, characteristics, abilities and traits that an employer is looking for in a supervisor or manager.

In Chapter Six are the behavioral dimensions that we used or have seen other test providers use and there is more detailed information about them. If the test provider is using the current professional practices, you should know the behavioral dimensions you are going to be assessed on ahead of time.

Key Theme: How you are scored is one of the central strengths of an assessment center and why it is the gold standard in promotional testing: Every behavioral dimension is scored at least twice, in different exercises and by different assessors. That means you will have multiple "bites at the apple" or multiple chances to show your abilities.

We have often seen candidates leave an exercise discouraged because they felt they could have done better. Shrug that feeling off because there will be more opportunities to demonstrate your skills. Also, what you feel discouraged about may not even be the behavioral dimensions the assessors were scoring.

And that brings us to the last point:

7. "**Scoring**" is the empirical method that leads to the final and total score and is covered in detail in Chapter 6. Test providers have different processes and approaches to this. The current professional practice is the test provider should provide an explanation of the scoring process prior to the assessment center. A great scoring process begins with the training of the

assessors by the test provider on the scoring values and how to determine an individual score and ends when the scores from the exercises are combined together.

THE KEY THEMES IN REVIEW:

- ✓ Be yourself from the beginning, and do not act, pretend or say what you think the assessors want to hear.

- ✓ Be the supervisor or manager in an authentic and genuine way. Let all of your decisions, actions and explanations flow from that attitude.

- ✓ Know what the position is, get the formal Job Description or other documents that describe the major duties and use these to direct your preparation. Talk to those in the position and learn what they really do and why.

- ✓ The assessors can only score you on what you say and do. They cannot assume, predict or interpret the meaning or reasons behind your actions and decisions in the exercises. Fully explain yourself in detail while being time aware.

- ✓ Behavioral dimensions are generally scored at least twice by different assessors and in different exercises. You will have multiple opportunities to demonstrate your skills and abilities. Study what the behavioral dimensions are.

✓ We have often seen candidates leave an exercise discouraged because they felt they could have done better. Shrug that feeling off because there will be more opportunities to demonstrate your skills. Also, what you feel discouraged about may not even be the behavioral dimensions the assessors were scoring.

Chapter 3

What To Expect On Test Day

The notion behind covering this topic now is to reduce your anxiety because this will help you learn the material that is presented later and you will be better prepared on test day. There are legitimate topics and questions to be understandably nervous about, however, the topics that follow **should not** be on that list. Being prepared for what will likely happen at the test will allow you to be more confident and allow you to focus on your performance during the job simulations.

The test provider should be able to provide you information on attire, where the testing process will be conducted, what time to report, and generally how long the testing event will last. Let's discuss these.

ATTIRE

Typically, the agency drives what attire the candidates will wear. In our experience, the majority of agencies choose business attire. Business attire for men is typically a suit with long sleeve shirt and tie. A suit is not slacks and a sports jacket. Business attire for women is typically a pants suit or skirt, blouse and a jacket.

Police agencies are traditionally conservative and therefore your clothing should be conservative in nature; darker colors for suites are typical and the style is conventional. One advantage to darker colors is they do not show dirt or stains. If you spilled water on dark pants, it would not be seen. Jewelry should be tasteful and minimal. The dress shirt is typically light colored that is crisp and pressed. The tie should complement the outfit nicely and the knot should be perfect. If you are not clothing conscious, consider using a personal shopper and going to a reputable store that has a professional staff. Then, accept their advice and try on a variety of looks and styles.

The goal is to look professional and be confident. Dress like you are the supervisor or manager. What are your agency's values about acceptable clothing? Your leadership team models those values everyday. Watch, look, and take note. The clothing you select should make you feel good, strong and prepared. The outfit is comfortable and helps you get through a stressful day. Strongly consider buying new clothing for the testing process because the clothing will be in excellent condition, the style will be current, the fit will be good, and you will have made a strong gesture of your commitment to do well.

Key Theme: Your attire is your first impression to the assessors; it creates the starting point for scoring. This is a powerful dynamic that you have control over.

The assessors are often in business attire and they will have the confidence and experience of wearing it well. Assessors can often not help their tendency to give higher scores to people whom they like. When they detect that you look good and are comfortable and professional in your attire, they are more apt to like you.

If the attire is uncomfortable and weighs you down, it may affect your performance. Marginal candidates are often easy to spot because they have put little thought into the impact of their appearance. Their clothing will be worn, ill fitting, their necktie is poorly tied or not aligned and they show their discomfort and dislike for their clothing.

The top tier candidates typically look sharp and professional. Shirts are pressed, ties are properly knotted, socks match the shoes and pants, and shoes are highly shined. Even when the attire is business casual and the agency is allowing slacks and a polo shirt, the serious candidate who is thinking like a supervisor will put a lot of effort into their appearance and attire.

For example, we tested 8 candidates for a Corrections Lieutenant in a county jail. The attire was advertised as business casual. The four candidates in the morning wore suits and ties. The four candidates in the afternoon wore casual slacks and open neck polo shirts that were authorized by their agency. All of the morning candidates outcompeted the afternoon candidates. The morning candidates were more serious, more focused and better prepared and their attire reflected those traits.

When the agency chooses their uniform as the attire, there should be clear direction on what that means and what your options are. If there is little direction, ask questions. Most agencies will choose the long sleeve formal uniform with a tie. If you are given a choice, the formal uniform is more impressive than the field uniform. If you have been in a non-uniform assignment for a while, do not assume that the uniform hanging in your closet will fit perfectly. You want to be impressive and demonstrating that includes having an impressive uniform. Assessors often cannot help but make the judgment that if you pay attention to the details of your appearance, you will pay attention to the important details of work. The assessors often model the performance that they want in others.

Consider having your formal uniform tailored to fit you perfectly. This is a small expense that will help you feeling more confident and sends a powerful message to the assessors before you say anything. Officers and deputies who have been members of their Honor Guard are practiced at looking very sharp. Make the effort to learn from them.

There may be instructions to NOT wear medals or other performance-earned insignia, as this does not create a level playing field among all the candidates. Some agencies will ask that nametags or years of service markings be removed or covered up so the assessors will not know the candidate's name or their years of experience. Why? Because there may be unconscious bias or pre-judging based upon this information. Again, these are topics and questions that should be addressed prior to the test day with the test provider.

Pay attention to your hair, face and hands. Get a fresh haircut or style and wear this in a manner that means you are ready to be the supervisor today. Your face and hands should be clean, styled, nails cleaned and trimmed that show your best efforts. You will be seated across a table from the assessors for 20 to 30 minutes and they will be focused on your torso, hands, face and hair. Stay away from scented products. Tattoos should be covered. Facial jewelry should be removed. Again, your agency's team of supervisors, managers and executives model what is expected in attire and appearance. Take a close look and make your decisions to fit into this team.

WHAT TO BRING

Candidates for law enforcement agencies may be asked to NOT bring firearms or handcuffs to the test. Besides the obvious reasons for this, sometimes the facility that is being used for the testing process does not have the chairs that can accommodate candidates who are wearing their duty gear. The good test provider will have considered the facility's chairs and addressed this issue. Having to battle uncomfortable chairs is a preventable source of stress for the candidates and is annoying to the assessors.

Typically, you do not bring anything - no notebooks, no resume, and no pens. Why? These can be opportunities to bring prohibited material to the test and unfortunately, there are a few candidates who will try to cheat. Typically, you will get all the materials and supplies that you will need on test day from the test provider.

Resumes are typically **not** allowed, because the assessors will only score you on what you say and do during the exercise and usually there is no time or place for a resume. The exception is for the position of command and where the assessors may see your resume before meeting you. The test provider will tell you to bring a resume and will often set the limitations such as two to three pages. If there is no instruction to bring one, do not bring a resume.

Unless you are on-call, do not bring a cell phone or any electronic devices into the test site. Receiving outside assistance is strictly prohibited. If you need to have a cell phone with you, it will be left with the test administrator.

Occasionally, a testing process may include an exercise that will involve work that you prepared before the test day. When these are brought to the test site, the test administrator will visually check them and may hold on to them until you go to that exercise.

Typically, light snacks and beverages are provided by the agency at the test site for the candidates. For all-day events, lunch is generally provided. However, we have seen agencies that will not provide any food to the candidates. Can you bring your own food or drink? These and other questions are topics that should be asked of the test provider before the test day.

Key Theme: The test provider should address the topics of attire and what to bring before test day. These are questions that you should proactively ask about.

HOW YOU START THE TEST SETS THE TONE

Enter the test site a few minutes before your scheduled reporting time. That means you got to the site with ample time to spare, knew where to park, made the last checks of clothing and appearance, and have the mental attitude you want. The top candidate will have test driven to the site, checked out the facilities before test day and made sure their car had enough fuel to get to the test. All of this preparation reduces anxiety and allows more energy for focusing on the actual test.

The marginal candidate will not have done this level of preparation. They will either arrive with moments to spare or will arrive too early and have too much time to kill. Either way, they get off on the wrong foot and are stressed, which affects their performance; all of this is preventable. Being late to the test is generally not allowed and the candidate is disqualified.

Your attitude and mindset about the test is an extremely powerful force. This is the primary trait that separates the top candidates from the rest. Consider the mindset that the promotional process begins when you get out of your car. Have the attitude and the mental and emotional disposition that you planned for and decided on in your preparation. This was said before because it is important, "**Think like and be the supervisor or manager**."

Key Theme: Be confident, calm, ready, and show that you are the leader **and** have the passion to do the job. This kind of mindset is another way of being committed to being at the top of your game.

You also want your sleep, blood sugar and caffeine levels where you want them. When the biology of these factors goes the wrong way, they will overwhelm your preparation. We saw a candidate who crammed for the test for three days with little sleep. He entered the test site looking rumbled and anxious. By the end of the four exercises, he was numb from exhaustion and had earned low scores.

Typically, there will be signs or personal guides at the test site to direct you to the Candidate's Room. Usually, this room will often have individual tables or assigned seating for each candidate that creates a workspace or office. Here you will do the prep work before each exercise and when an exercise is over, return to your workspace. Often beverages and light snacks will be in this room.

Usually the Candidate's Room is a quiet place if anyone is working. If no one is working, then candidates can socialize appropriately, provided the topics are not test related. The Test Administrator often works from the Candidate's Room and will act to prevent any gamesmanship and enforce the rules of the testing process.

Key Theme: The top tier candidate will be acting and thinking like the supervisor or manager the entire time while at the test site.

THE CANDIDATE'S BRIEFING

The briefing begins with determining the letter designator for each candidate. The test administrator will have a process for the candidates to be assigned a letter identifier. Candidates will wear a badge with their letter for the entire testing process. Why a letter? This is a continuation of the notion of a level playing field for all candidates. Names and titles can create a positive or negative bias. Also, every piece of paper that you handle will need your candidate letter. The assessors will know you by your candidate letter and will have only your candidate letter on their score sheet.

Then, the candidates will sign-in on a roster that corresponds to the candidate letter. The sign-in will include both a signature and a printed name. A photo will be taken of each candidate with the candidate's letter being visible. The photo will marry the candidate's face to their candidate letter for documentation. The assessors will use the photos to remember each candidate as they talk about the performance they observed and heard.

The formal briefing by the Test Administrator will typically start with the distribution of each candidate's schedule of the exercises. Usually, you will know the number of exercises before the test and the schedule will correspond to that number. Sometimes an exercise is divided up into pieces that assessors will evaluate and the schedule will reflect that. The schedule usually has the time, the length of the prep time and the exercise and the exercise number but does not name or describe it. Typically, you will not know what the exercise is until you receive the prep materials at the time listed on your schedule.

In a typical assessment center of eight candidates, up to four candidates will start in the morning and four more will start in the afternoon. Many test vendors have a strict guideline that limits the number of candidates per day because more candidates will push the schedule much longer and the fatigue of the assessors can cause lower scores for the candidates. Each schedule is unique because of the number of exercises, the length of the exercises and the number of candidates.

We have not found a relationship between the top scoring candidate and what time of day they started or on what day they tested. If the assessors and role players have enough time to work effectively and if periodic rest and refreshments are available, their scoring remains strong and consistent, regardless of the time of day.

Usually, test providers will try to minimize the wait time between exercises to about 10 to 25 minutes. There are many factors that go into building a test day schedule and sometimes longer wait times cannot be avoided. Most of the time candidates are testing for about half a day. The test provider should be able to tell you in advance how long the test will take. Testing that exceeds 8 hours a day will exhaust both the candidate and the assessor. Unless working while exhausted is in the Job Description, this may be grounds for an appeal of the test.

The test administrator will give the final briefing that includes the rules and other topics. Candidates will usually have a copy of the briefing to follow along and will be asked to sign it, acknowledging that they understand the information presented.

The typical topics of the briefing and the rules are:

- Who the test staff are and how they are identified,

- The number of scored exercises and how many candidates are testing,

- If there are observers, you will be told in advance who they are and that they have no influence in scoring,

- Assume that you are working the position being tested for with all the duties, responsibilities and authority that the position has,

- No devices or materials that are not provided can be used during the test,

- Receiving assistance or accessing outside resources during the test is prohibited,

- Do not interact with the assessors or role players outside of the exercise,

- Revealing information about this test to any other candidate, who has not experienced it, is prohibited,

- If you recognize an assessor and feel they cannot grade you fairly, go through the exercise, and contact the test provider immediately following the exercise,

- Grading for each exercise will begin when you enter the room and/or when you are instructed to start,

- The names of the role players and other employees in this assessment center are fictitious. Any similarity to a real person or situation is coincidental, and

- The assessors can only score you on what you say and do. They cannot predict or interpret based on your prior experience, training or other qualifications.

THE KEY THEMES IN REVIEW:

- ✓ Your attire is your first impression to the assessors; it creates the starting point of scoring. This is a powerful dynamic that you have control over.

- ✓ The test provider should address the topics of attire and what to bring before test day. These are questions that you should proactively ask about.

- ✓ Be confident, calm, ready, and show that you are the leader and have the passion to do the job. This kind of mindset is another way of being committed to being at the top of your game.

- ✓ Days before the test visit the site; know your route, where to park and plan the timing so you have a comfortable amount of time to get your head in the game.

- ✓ On test day, have your rest, blood sugar and caffeine levels where you want them.

- ✓ Be the supervisor or manager for the entire time while at the test site.

- ✓ Know the rules of the testing process and follow them.

Chapter 4

The Testing Process

Each exercise or job simulation at an assessment center typically has a preparation time before the exercise and a presentation time with the assessors. Understanding these and being successful at each of these is important. Let's talk about the <u>preparation time</u> and then break down the <u>presentation time</u> with the assessors into its components.

PREPARATION TIME

The preparation time is for you to study and work before meeting with the assessors. Your behavior is not scored during the preparation time. The amount of that time may be as short as 5 minutes and may be as long as hours. For example, some critical thinking-decision making exercises have only a 5-minute prep time because there is not much to prepare for as you will receive only a skeleton amount of information about an unfolding scenario that needs to be assessed and acted on. The longest prep times are typically writing exercises, such as you will write a memorandum or a number of emails. The most common preparation times are 10 to 15 minutes.

The test administrator will distribute the test's prep materials at a specific time and you will have them for a specific duration of time.

Typically, the prep work is done in the Candidate's Room where you will have access to pens, pencils, highlighters, and a note pad. Some test vendors have a candidate preparation area for every exercise where you will be alone with the materials. When the instructions and materials are printed, you can mark these up with notes and emphasize certain points.

Though you cannot bring anything into the testing process, you can make notes to yourself in the Candidate Room. Top candidates will often write down the messages that they want to give to the assessors, self-coaching hints to use, or important information like the agency's key parts of the mission, values, and vision.

Key Theme: Use these reminders and personal instructions throughout the test day and with every exercise to help stay focused and to keep the attitude of being the supervisor.

Typically, the prep materials can be taken into the exercise room for you to refer to because this is what generally happens on the job; prepare for the meeting, bring your notes and you can refer to them. After the exercise, take all of these back to the Candidate's Room and return them to the Test Administrator, where they will be shredded.

Key Theme: Typically, the assessors and your employer will not see your notes because you are only assessed on what you say and do in the exercise room during the assessment process. This is a topic that should be asked about prior to the test.

Usually, the test administrator will not give you a warning when the prep time is almost over. Therefore, you should wear a watch to monitor your time. You will not be able to use a cell phone to keep track of time. The test administrator will end the prep time and take you to the exercise room at the proper time.

PRESENTATION TIME: THE EXERCISE ROOM WITH THE ASSESSORS

The better test vendors will tell you how the room is laid out behind the closed door, where the assessors are, if there is an observer, who they are and where they are, and if there is a role player in the room and where they are. This is done so you are prepared; that there are no preventable surprises and every candidate starts with the same information.

Many times we have been in a church for the testing process because these have the space and are often at low or no cost to the agency. Sometimes the spaces used for the exercise have religious related themes on the walls. Do not be distracted by these. Rather, prepare and accept them knowing that they have no relation to the testing process.

The furniture in the exercise room will be laid out to fit the exercise. When there is a role player, we typically put two tables in a T-formation with the assessors at the top of the T. That way, the assessors have a clear view of the participants and can easily hear both sides of the conversation. When the exercise is just the candidate and the assessors, typically two tables are put together to make one double-wide table as this creates the right conversation distance while having enough work space for the assessor's materials and the candidate's materials. When there are multiple role-players, such as a shift briefing or community presentation, the room will be laid out to try to be similar to the workplace. For these exercises, the assessors are often seated behind the role players so they have a full view of the candidate.

Key Theme: Be sure you can be seen and heard by the assessors.

For exercises with role players, can you move your chair and alter the room setup? Absolutely, because this is an option in the workplace. In fact, moving chairs from a frontal face-to-face design to chairs at right angles to each other or being side by side can be a very effective non-verbal strategy; one that is not lost on the role player or the assessors. Being the supervisor can mean putting the other person at ease and being less confrontational. The caveat is the assessors need to have an excellent vantage point to see and hear the conversation. The assessors are running the exercise and they may react to changes in the room setup accordingly.

If the exercise uses technology, such as watching a PowerPoint program, the screen and the speakers will be where you should sit.

Your non-verbal language will always speak louder than the words you chose. Your posture while seated is part of the message. Sit up straight with a posture that shows your interest, professionalism and being engaged. Keep your hands and arms on top of the table. Take a tip from television personalities on how to sit: divide the seat in half and sit on the front half and your body will naturally move to the correct posture with your feet flat on the floor and supporting you with your shoulders over your hips.

Candidates who sit back in the chair will often cross their legs and then give the demeanor of being too casual, not serious, and not listening; the lower scores will reflect this non-verbal message.

STARTING THE EXERCISE

What about introducing yourself to the assessors? Absolutely, if it is appropriate for the exercise. Just because you are wearing a letter badge, does not mean that you have left your identity and personality behind. If it is comfortable and appropriate, tell the assessors your name, make genuine eye contact and shake their hand. This is not appropriate when role-players are in the room and the job simulation begins when you enter the room. It would feel odd and would be inappropriate to ignore role-players, walk past them and introduce yourself to the assessors and then begin the scenario. This would be contrary to the exercise's instructions, would catch the assessors by surprise and would likely lead to lower scores.

Typically, when a role-player is not in the room at the beginning of an exercise, the assessors will briefly introduce the exercise by reading a few bullet points from their instructions. This information is typically repeated from the written instructions that you received in the prep area but it sets the tone and after reading the introduction, the timer will be started and the exercise begins.

The scoring begins either when you enter the exercise room and meet the role player(s) who are waiting for you or after the assessors have introduced the exercise and started the timer.

USING YOUR PRESENTATION TIME WISELY

The amount of allotted time with the assessors is described in the instructions that you received in the prep area. Typically, the time ranges from 20 to 30 minutes. You are held to this time but you are in control of how you use it. Sometimes, and the instructions should tell you, the assessors will give a warning that time is expiring.

The marginal candidate's narratives are either very, very short or very long and disorganized. These candidates are often unaware of the time. Some candidates will speak so fast because they are often in fear of running out of time. Fear is your enemy during the testing process because it will crack your confidence and inhibit your ability to show your skills and knowledge. If you feel afraid, stop, take a breath and re-focus by remembering that you are the supervisor.

The long-winded candidates often have lower scoring because they are so caught up with their story that they forget about time. These candidates will either over-talk a topic by telling distracting sub-stories or will ramble, hoping that something they have said will earn points.

The top tier candidate will pace themselves, are aware of their time, cover the important points while providing the supporting evidence, and deliver their presentation using their best oral communication skills. They will use nearly all of their time because they have planned their narrative, are comfortable because they are prepared, and are not nervous because they know themselves.

An effective strategy to being time aware is to carefully note the time when the assessors start the their timer. Make this notation on the instructions or on your notes that you can easily see. Then, casually glance at your watch as the exercise progresses, adjusting your narrative accordingly and staying true to the priorities of your messages.

Key Theme: Higher scoring candidates will use the appropriate time to fully explain and provide the assessors with complete information that explains the *reasons, values, and principles behind their actions.* They view **time** as an opportunity, not an obstacle, to demonstrate their skills.

WHAT ELSE?

Typically, you will go to different locations for each exercise and will meet different assessors at each one. Because each exercise and job simulation is assessed by at least two assessors, if there are four exercises you will meet at least 8 different assessors.

Key Theme: Each exercise and job simulation is scored independently of the other exercises and by different assessors. Therefore, you have new opportunities at each exercise and job simulation to demonstrate your knowledge, skills and abilities. The strong candidate will not let their perception of how they did in one event affect their performance in others.

The assessors will give you little or no feedback during the exercise. They will be trained to be neutral and professional.

Often, there is little or no eye contact because the assessors are writing notes, typing on a laptop and consulting their instructions and the scoring guidelines to your narrative. The candidate who is unprepared for this lack of feedback will often become uncertain and may lose confidence and this will affect their performance. The top candidate will anticipate and prepare for this lack of connection with the assessors and will adapt and overcome it.

Whether the exercise is the In-Basket or a critical thinking & decision-making event, the job simulation or exercise is often a monologue with no give and take with the assessors. This is an unusual communication dynamic that you may not be experienced at and is common at an assessment center. Speaking for three minutes will feel like 20 minutes. Staying focused on the sequence of the message and covering the important points, while sounding interesting, can be very difficult. Therefore, commit to something that few other candidate will do: practice delivering a 20 minute long monologue with someone while being recorded by video camera and then carefully and honesty critique yourself. Here are some topics and questions to ask yourself:

- Write down three topics that you know a lot about. Then with the video on, have your off-screen partner select one of the topics. This is you talking about something you are comfortable with. Do look and sound like a person who has a depth of information and interest?

- Nervousness should be minimal for the above topic. What are your non-verbal mannerisms that are distracting? What are the words and phrases that are your "fillers?"

- Write down three topics that you should know about but are weak in. Then with the video rolling, your off-screen partner will select one. This is you struggling and thinking in front of the camera. Are you cool, in control and professional? Do you maintain eye contact?

- Examine your posture and what your body is doing while you are speaking. These messages are louder than the words that you use. You want to be calm, focused, centered and in the moment with your message.

- Doing the video will show the gap between what you think you do and what you actually do. Everyone has a gap but the questions are, are you self-aware of the differences, are willing to adapt and is your gap as narrow as possible?

The marginal candidate is unprepared for speaking without feedback and will tire after two or three minutes of talking. They will become disorganized, will repeat themselves and will become discouraged. Discouragement will destroy the best delivery of communication and the assessors will detect this attitude and will give lower scores.

At the end of the day, you will be exhausted and emotionally spent. The top scoring candidates are prepared for this and will pace themselves to finish well. The lower scoring candidates will not have the same energy for the last exercise as they did for the first one. The assessors may perceive this because the candidate's delivery is flat and uninteresting and the assessors may conclude that the candidate does not have the passion or enthusiasm for the promotion.

Before you leave the test site you may be asked to complete a brief survey about your experience. This provides feedback about that agency's choice of exercises and gives ideas on how to improve the process.

Better test providers will allow the assessors to create a set of commendations or positive messages about what you did well and recommendations about what you can improve on. These comments are not tied to your score and are personal messages from the assessors to you. These test providers will take these raw comments, re-format them into one document and send them to the agency and they will give them to you. More about these are in Chapter Seven.

It is not unusual that the agency will receive the raw scores immediately and often before the test provider leaves the test site. The release of the final scores is done by your agency in a matter and time that follows their rules and procedures.

THE KEY THEMES IN REVIEW:

- ✓ Wear a watch so you can monitor your time,

- ✓ Study the schedule so you know all the elements and you can pace yourself through the whole test,

- ✓ Make notes and mark up any material given to you in the prep area and use these in the exercise to keep on track and cover your points,

- ✓ Create your own personal reminders and private instructions that can be used throughout the test day and with every exercise to help stay focused and to keep the attitude of being the supervisor.

✓ Listen carefully to the Test Administrator at the exercise site and before entering visualize how the room is laid out so you are more comfortable.

✓ Use your posture to convey confidence,

✓ Make certain that the assessors can hear you during the exercise,

✓ Higher scoring candidates will use the appropriate time to fully explain and provide the assessors with complete information that explains the *reasons, values, and principles behind their actions.* They view **time** as an opportunity, not an obstacle, to demonstrate their skills.

✓ Each exercise and job simulation is scored independently of the other exercises and by different assessors. Therefore, you have "multiple bites at the apple." Do not let your perception of how you did in one event affect the others.

✓ Know the rules and the timing of the release of the final scores to avoid needless anxiety and respect the work of the agency's human resources staff and their process.

Chapter 5

The Assessors & Role Players

An assessment center looks like an orchestrated collision between qualified candidates, trained assessors and job-related exercises that are valid, objective and defensible. This chapter will discuss the assessors, who they are and how they are typically trained. The bulk of the chapters that follow will discuss the families of exercises that you may experience, what great candidates look like, the mistakes that are commonly made and how to prepare.

One of the obstacles facing an agency that wants to conduct an assessment center is finding enough qualified assessors. Many test providers ask the agency to find the assessors while some other test providers will provide the assessors. Most of the time, the agency knows best the qualifications of the assessors they want and will select the most qualified assessors that understand their agency, the environment the agency works in, the context of the position and knows the professional experience and reputation of the assessors that they want.

Nearly all test providers only use assessors from outside the agency hosting the test because these assessors can be more objective. When an assessor comes from the candidate's agency, it is very difficult to defend against the challenge of bias. How can the inside assessor prove that the candidate's score did not include prior knowledge of the candidate's performance? Also, when there is an assessor from the candidate's agency, often the outside assessors are influenced and even persuaded by this assessor's judgments and adjust their scores.

The occasional exception is when the candidate is asked to present an oral resume of their training, education, accomplishments and professional qualifications. Sometimes, a member of the candidate's agency is present as a resource to the assessors and does not participate in scoring or offer an opinion. Rather, they have the responsibility of verifying that what the candidate described or took credit for actually happened.

The presence of this "truth-seeker" can be a powerful force in reducing bragging. For example, we saw a candidate make a convincing presentation that took credit for creating new programs, salvaged an under-performing employee, and improved moral on their team. The agency's truth-seeker told the assessors that all this was simply not the case and this resulted in the candidate receiving very low scores. The lesson here is clear: never, ever misrepresent yourself, make stuff up or embellish. The better test provider will tell you before an exercise that a member of your agency is present.

Unlike most other promotional processes, in an assessment center, the ratio of assessors to candidates may be closer to one-to-one. Each exercise will need at least two assessors; three is better and occasionally an agency will have four assessors per exercise. So, be ready to meet at least 8 assessors at a four-exercise assessment center.

WHO ARE THE ASSESSORS & ROLE PLAYERS

Assessors are generally veteran supervisors or managers who have volunteered to help the agency. They are experienced and knowledgeable supervisors, managers and executives from like-agencies who are the same rank or higher than the position being tested for. Many test providers use assessors from the same region as the client agency and may even be neighbors.

Most of the assessors have done this before. When there are new assessors, they are partnered with experienced ones. Better test providers will give the experienced assessors new exercises so they do not unintentionally bring their biases from another assessment center experience into this promotional process. When several assessors come from the same agency, they are split up. The test provider should spread the ranks of assessors into different exercises, meaning there will likely be assessors of different ranks in each exercise. The underlying principle is to have a diverse group of assessors at every exercise because this diversity brings different perspectives and therefore creates a richer score.

We have also had excellent experience with veteran managers from other government departments, the private sector, and retired managers and executives. These assessors will be partnered with an assessor from law enforcement. If the exercise is very technical in nature, then the assessors will only be from police agencies.

Most of the assessors are volunteers who want to participate and they are not receiving any additional financial benefit other than their normal salary. Their agency is helping your agency with the hope that the favor will be returned in the future. A few test providers pay assessors and will use them repeatedly.

Role players are generally line employees or first-line supervisors who have volunteered to be a role player to experience the assessor training and the promotional testing process. Often, the role players will attend the assessor training and this adds to their professional development. Occasionally, an agency will use a professional actor or a member of the community who has a talent for being a role player.

Role players and assessors are usually screened to prevent those who have a relationship with any of the candidates. Though some role players are stronger than others, we have not experienced any who were less than adequate. Perhaps the reason for this is the detail in which their character is developed and the care and direction provided by the test provider and assessors who are running the exercise.

Key Theme: Assessors and role players share the common value of wanting to participate and to help the agency choose the best candidate possible.

TRAINING THE ASSESSORS AND ROLE PLAYERS

The test provider will send the assessors some information

about the position and portions of the assessor's training manual before attending the assessor training. The training is typically at least three hours long and some test providers will train for an entire day. This training often occurs the day before the assessment center or the morning of the first day. The topics include much of what is included in this book and much of the information in the handouts we have used is included here.

By the end of the training, the group will understand what the position is, the basics of the organization, how the testing process will be administered, what the behavioral dimensions are, what successful candidates look like, and practice scoring the behavioral dimensions and applying the scoring values. Then, the assessors will break up into their exercises to study and practice. The role players will practice their part repeatedly until they are comfortable with their character.

The assessors have the responsibility to run their exercise within the parameters of their training and will work with the testing staff and the subject matter expert to know and adjust the exercise to make it as effective as possible.

On test day, the assessors and role players are fully prepared, excited and ready for you.

WHAT HAPPENS ON TEST DAY

The assessors will typically be wearing business attire. Role players will be wearing clothing suitable for their character. That means if a role player is an employee, they may be wearing the uniform shirt of your agency. Usually, all the names of the role players are fictitious. If a name is familiar to you, it is totally by accident. The role players wear a distinctive nametag with their character's name on it. The intention is that you will not need to memorize their name from the prep material. Again, there are lots of things to be nervous about at an assessment center, memorizing a role player's name should not be one of them.

Role players are provided a character with some biographical background, the reasons behind their behavior and emotions, and the boundaries of their behavior and conversation to stay in. During the assessor training they will practice their role and receive coaching and guidance to further develop their character. Role players will start the exercise with every candidate the same way with the same demeanor and same opening line. Then they will react to you, given the goals of the exercise and the boundaries they have.

Meeting with a role player about a topic is just like real life. You will have some information that was provided in the prep area, but this information is generally incomplete and the role player will often have new information for you. Top candidates remember that communication is a two-way process of giving information and asking questions but also carefully listening to the responses. Marginal candidates will have lower listening skills and therefore miss important information. Worse, they will not ask questions and will have made a rigid judgment using only the information provided in the prep area.

Besides the important skill of listening and gathering new information, the other skill is making an on-the-spot decision in front of the assessors. Top candidates will demonstrate their intellect, their knowledge of policy, procedure and principle, and their courage and strength to make a decision and to communicate it.

Key Theme: Top tier candidates view a role-play job simulation as being real and will apply their skills and abilities effectively.

The community of policing is really not that big. There is the possibility that when you enter an exercise room, you may recognize or perhaps know or have heard of an assessor or role player. Though the test provider may work at preventing this, this sometimes happens. Therefore, do not interact with an assessor or a role player outside of the exercise room because doing so sends the message to anyone watching that the playing field is not level.

Key Theme: If you recognize an assessor or role player that you know, do not acknowledge that relationship. The assessors and the role players will be trained to do the same.

What if you know an assessor and are concerned that they will not judge you fairly based on bad history or bias? Ask the test provider about that. Be prepared to go through the exercise to the best of your ability. Then, immediately tell the test administrator or another staff member after the exercise, because there is often a method that can be used to watch the scores behind the scenes for evidence of bias. Should that happen, the agency's human resources staff will be monitoring and will keep in touch with you about the outcome.

The assessors are trained to not use profanity, get in your face or treat you in any way that is rude or demeaning, but they may ask difficult and pointed questions. However, the role players are different. Do supervisors and managers deal with difficult people who may be upset? The role players will not touch you or act in a manner that requires the use of force or to make an arrest but they may be loud, rude and use profanity.

> Seek out opportunities to be a role-player as part of your preparation to be a supervisor and a top tier candidate.

The assessors have the latitude to ask clarifying questions should a candidate use a word or phrase whose meaning is unknown to them. Therefore, do not be surprised that an assessor interrupts your narrative with a question. The question is intended for better understanding, not to throw you off-balance. Obviously, the way to prevent this is to not use words or phrases that are unique to your agency and to fully explain yourself.

THE KEY THEMES IN REVIEW:

- ✓ Assessors are typically professionals, who want to participate in the process, will give their full attention and want candidates to succeed.

- ✓ Assessor and role players will be trained and will feel comfortable with their exercise. The assessors will be running the exercise.

- ✓ Role players will have distinctive nametags to identify them as role players and you do not have to memorize their name.

- ✓ View role-play job simulations as being real. Take it seriously and apply all of your skill set to the scenario.

✓ If you recognize someone you know, do not acknowledge that relationship because doing so sends the message to anyone watching that the playing field is not level for all the candidates.

✓ The assessors are trained to be friendly but neutral and professional. Be ready for no feedback from them as they often spend their time documenting what you say and do.

✓ Seek out opportunities to be a role-player as part of your preparation to be a supervisor and a top tier candidate.

Chapter 6

Behavioral Dimensions and What Is Being Evaluated

The number one question that candidates asked us is, "What am I evaluated on?" Asked another way but the same topic is, "What are the assessors looking for?" The answers to those questions are what this chapter is about.

During each exercise or job simulation, the assessors will be categorizing many of your actions and words into the behavioral dimensions that are provided by the test provider. A "behavioral dimension" is a term that is used in promotional testing and means: a collection of measureable characteristics or traits that describe a candidate's performance and are grouped under one heading.

For example, the behavioral dimension of Oral Communication could include the specific topics of word usage, mastery of the technical information, persuasiveness, confidence, volume, clarity of speech, non-verbal language, quality of the message, command presence, active listening skills, organization of the message, and public speaking skills.

Behavioral dimensions are used in assessment centers because it allows for a greater depth and a broader spectrum of assessment. Many, many measurable characteristics can be grouped into less than a dozen behavioral dimensions that are assessed during the assessment center.

Perhaps, you noticed the difficulty in scoring a behavioral dimension when there are a host of topics within the dimension. Using the example of Oral Communication, how does the assessor score this when the candidate does really well at public speaking skills but poorly at active listening skills? The take-away is this important point:

Key Theme: Broaden your strengths into as many topics as possible. Accept the coaching that though you are strong in some areas, there are always areas that need further development. Many times, our weakness are an **overuse of a strength,** for example, strong listening skills can lead to the perception of being too quiet and reserved.

Though you want to prepare for every behavioral dimension and will strive to do your best to earn the highest scores in each, most candidates will excel in some and will be weaker in others. As you study the behavioral dimensions, do your own internal assessment on each. What are your strong areas? Which ones do you struggle with?

Now, take a page from a Music Director who has built and rose up through the performances of orchestras. His strategy for accomplishing this was to work on the weaker areas of the group, and then the whole orchestra would sound better. If public speaking is your weakness, then take the time and the effort to practice and be better. Conversely, if you are a natural people-person, who genuinely cares about people and your listening skills are well developed, do not spend a huge effort on developing your interpersonal insight. Fight the temptation to do only the easy work.

Marginal candidates will often earn a higher score in only one behavioral dimension. Stronger candidates have higher scores in at least half of the behavioral dimensions and the top tier candidates will have only one or maybe two behavioral dimensions that are not very strong. To be clear, strong scores do not mean having the best score; it means having the number one, two or three score in **every one** of the behavioral dimensions.

Experience is everything because it is the best teacher. Candidates who have a wider variety of experiences often earn higher scores because they can see the bigger picture and the ramifications and interconnectedness of their actions. Their deep well of experiences has yielded many lessons from both mistakes and successes. Good candidates will study and memorize the academic or the science of supervision and management. The top candidates will have built upon this knowledge with personal experience.

To illustrate this, here are some examples:

1. The deputy sheriff who has spent their whole career in patrol. Though they are a master-level employee at what they do, they have no depth of experience at investigations or at a tactical event that uses a lot of resources and lasts for hours. The candidate did not prepare for this and during the assessment center, the candidate stumbled and was uncertain.

The opposite is also true. The long-time detective did poorly on a job simulation that involved supervising multiple events and prioritizing calls for service.

2. The Lieutenant who spent the last four years in an administrative assignment and not supervising anyone did poorly in an employee counseling exercise because they were not as experienced with providing clear performance expectations and creating a plan to monitor progress. This was preventable if the candidate had focused their preparation on their weaker areas.

3. The employee who is the long-time leader of the union realized that their perception of the agency leadership was not balanced. This candidate studied, sought out honest feedback, and found a coach to help them develop the perspective and attitude to be a top candidate.

4. The mid-manager who has spent many years handling and supervising the investigations of complaints against employees with the collateral assignment of maintaining the agency's accreditation status. The candidate could not do the full spectrum of duties and responsibilities, especially community engagement meetings and managing a critical event. During the assessment center, they looked at every situation through their current lens and the result was a marginal score. When all you have is a hammer, everything looks like a nail.

5. The deputy sheriff who has worked patrol, been a field training officer, a detective, an acting supervisor and has been

a part of a committee that accomplished a large project. This candidate did well in most of the behavioral dimensions but did not have the best score in any of them, and yet still came out in the top tier of candidates.

Key Theme: You do not have to have the best score in a behavioral dimension to be in the top tier of candidates. You need to have a consistently higher score in all of the behavioral dimensions. The most well rounded candidate that has the widest and most complete skill set and the best attitude will ultimately have the highest score. Being well rounded occurs through experience and preparation.

Typically, each exercise will have three to five behavioral dimensions that are designed and assigned by the test provider for scoring and each exercise or job simulation will have a different combination of behavioral dimensions to be assessed. You will not know which of the behavioral dimensions that the assessors are scoring in the exercise. Remember, the behavioral dimensions are typically scored at least twice, in different exercises, and therefore by different assessors and that is the central strength of an assessment center.

The assessors will be categorizing the relevant pieces of your performance, words and actions that you do into the behavioral dimensions. Most assessors will be making notes at a very fast rate to document what they see and hear.

> **The Key Theme:** If you do not effectively do or say it, you cannot receive credit for it. This is more than just content, it also how well you communicate. You could have a superior collection of experiences and training but if you cannot effectively communicate those to the assessors, the meaning may be lost. Usually, your education, training and experience is not known by the assessors and therefore it will not be given any credit in the scoring unless you talk about it.

The test provider usually offers the set of behavioral dimensions to the agency during the planning of the assessment center and should be able to justify their selection of the dimensions. Test providers generally use one of these schools of thought about using behavioral dimensions:

1. Use a smaller group of behavioral dimensions that are scored twice in different exercises. We have talked about this earlier and the strength is that you get "multiple bites at the same apple."

2. Use a larger group of behavioral dimensions where some are scored twice and others only once. The strength of this one is a broader span of traits is evaluated and more important ones can be scored twice.

Whichever approach is used, the behavioral dimensions need to fit the position being tested for and the agency. The current professional practice is the test provider should reveal the behavioral dimensions to you before the test.

Here are examples of behavioral dimensions for **first level supervision positions**:

Oral Communication	Delegation & Control
Written Communication	Customer Service
Interpersonal Insight	Teamwork
Problem Analysis	Decision Making & Problem
Judgment	Solving
Decisiveness	Job Knowledge
Planning & Organizing	Job Preparation

Behavioral dimensions naturally overlap; so do not be concerned when there is some duplication of characteristics. For example, where does Judgment end and Delegation & Control begin? Each panel of assessors will sort out this overlap in a manner that works for them and as long as the panel uses the same criteria with each candidate, this is rarely an issue.

Here are examples of behavioral dimensions for **command, management and executive positions**:

Initiative and Motivation	Leadership Skills
Interpersonal Relations	Communication Presentation
Communication Skills,	Skills
Management & Supervision	Adaptability/Flexibility
Performance Under Stress	Conflict Resolution
Leadership & Integrity	Creativity
Organizational & Technical	Emotional Intelligence
Skills	Persuasiveness
Management & Practical	Performance Management
Skills	Public Relations
Interpersonal Skills	Disciplinary Procedures

Command Character	Courage
Management Skills	Empathy
Vision	Passion
Trustworthiness	

Key Theme: Knowing what you are being evaluated on will help direct your preparation.

SCORING GUIDELINES FOR EACH BEHAVIORAL DIMENSION

Let's drill down on the most common behavioral dimensions and the associated guideposts or scoring guidelines that the assessors may use. This is useful because these could apply to most other behavioral dimensions that are offered by other test providers.

Each of the behavioral dimensions includes a definition and a scoring guideline to assist the assessors in their evaluating and scoring. The scoring guidelines for each behavioral dimension are a list of descriptions and behaviors that are divided into two categories: lower scoring and higher scoring candidates. The guidelines are not a standard or expectation, rather they are guidelines for the assessors. These are used to delineate and create consistent criteria for scoring.

Key Theme: For your professional development, use the "Traits of Lower Scoring Candidates" as a list of things to NOT do in your daily life and work. Use the "Traits of Higher Scoring Candidates" as a list to work on and build your set of skills and abilities.

ORAL COMMUNICATION

Definition: Effectiveness of expression in individual or group situations and includes verbal and non-verbal communication, active listening, explaining technical terms, and adapting to different audiences. Examples are public speaking, interviewing, counseling and teaching.

Traits Of Lower Scoring Candidates

- Wavers, uncertain, lacks confidence
- Arrogant, domineering, brash
- Nervousness that detracted from the presentation
- Poor verbal delivery affected the quality of the message
- Substantial non-verbal distracters from the verbal message
- No respect or trust to employees or citizen and little or none was earned
- Appearance or hygiene was substandard or distracting from the message
- Rambled, disjointed or disorganized
- Not sufficient explanation, glosses over, lacks reasonable detail
- No underlying values & principles
- Weak beginning or introduction
- Began with an inappropriate apology
- Ill prepared without facts and reasons
- Missed key points or made errors of fact

- Inappropriate words or phrases that reflected poorly on the agency
- Poor assessment of the audience, did not recognize their needs or agenda
- Little or no sympathy or empathy; poor social awareness
- Did not listen, only waited, was self-absorbed or distracted

Traits Of Higher Scoring Candidates

- Persuasive, engaging, interesting, likeable, inspiring
- Demonstrated effective command presence
- Self-controlled, disciplined
- Calm, confident, self-assured, polished
- Logical, reasonable, clear explanations
- Clear and articulate
- Adapted well to different settings and audiences
- Explanation was sound and reasonable
- Explained values & principles behind decisions, policies or practices
- Introduction summarized the main themes that are explained in detail later
- Supportive of the agency & their role in achieving the goals, mission & vision
- Presented facts and information to support themes
- Hit all or nearly all the key points
- Managed their presentation effectively without being too rushed or too short
- Good eye contact

- Accurately assessed the audience
- Demonstrated empathy; attuned to the feelings of another, good social awareness

WRITTEN COMMUNICATION

Definition: Organizes facts, clear and concise writing, can effectively critique other's writing, creates a quality product under a deadline. Examples are email, memorandum, report, and analysis with recommendations.

Traits Of Lower Scoring Candidates

- Four or more grammatical errors per page that detracted from the message such as wrong words, mixing tenses, wrong contractions, wrong genders, run-on sentences, poor paragraph construction or failed to use correct punctuation
- Vague, unclear or confusing message
- Missed significant errors or missing work in reviewing reports
- Left the reader with more than two un-answered major concerns or issues
- Incomplete work with substantial omissions
- Chaotic flow of the message that left the reader wondering
- Recommendations or opinions were not supported by analysis or facts

- Failed to adequately edit their work
- Overall product did not meet the normal and accepted minimum writing expectations of the profession
- Weak or no introduction
- Weak or no conclusion
- Visually, the writing looked confusing and unprofessional
- Omitted key facts
- Incorrect or wrong information
- Made up information, if not allowed in the instructions; penalty if the dimension of judgment is not scored here
- Work did not adequately stand-alone, leaving the reader with a need for more information
- Inconsistent information between what was written and what was orally presented

Traits Of Higher Scoring Candidates

- No grammar and spelling issues
- Discovered missing work that should have been done
- Clarity in sentence and paragraph structure
- Recommendations were supported by a compelling analysis of the facts
- Flow of the message was logical and effectively builds to a conclusion
- Sources of factual information were provided
- Complete product was produced within the time allowed
- Product met or exceeded the profession's expectations.
- Strong beginning or introduction

- Strong conclusion that summarized points
- Recommendations or position were strongly supported
- Visually pleasing
- Had all the main facts or issues
- A competent and professional stand-along product
- Consistency between what was written and what was orally presented

INTERPERSONAL INSIGHT

Definition: Effectively perceives and reacts to the needs of others and uses objectivity when perceiving the impact of oneself on others. Examples are coaching and counseling, dispute resolution, and citizen or employee complaint interview.

Traits Of Lower Scoring Candidates
- Clearly not a fit for the leadership team
- Took sides, showed partiality, jumped to conclusions
- Pretended to or did not fully listen to the other person as shown by non-verbal or verbal feedback: interrupted, talked-over, stoic, looked away
- Officious, domineering, arrogant, brazen, entitled, insensitive, abrasive or biased
- Dictated terms without full agreement or understanding by the other person
- Missed opportunities to identify areas for improvement by the employee or the agency
- Insensitive, disinterested in the other person

- Unable to recognize their own deficiencies
- Guarded, closed, aloof, disengaged
- Rigid in their approach
- Little or no mediation of conflict
- Stress-out, showed anger, frustration, inappropriate emotion
- Evasive, irritating, rambling
- Behaved in a less than ethical way
- Unaware of their impact on others
- Marginal representative of the agency & profession
- Written work: people were treated unfairly, mitigating information was omitted, recommendations or analysis were exaggerated or facts were minimized

Traits of Higher Scoring Candidates

- Displayed humility
- Like-able, genuine, warm, authentic
- Willingness to be open, be vulnerable
- Inspired respect and desire to follow
- Consistently communicated fairness, honesty and impartiality
- Can mediate a dispute
- Achieved understanding to improve a performance issue
- Proactively identified an issue that ultimately made a positive contribution
- Showed active listening, communicating understanding, and establishing rapport

- Their personal values are in-line with the agency and the profession
- Remained calm under stress; did not lose their temper or express frustration
- Was a calming influence on others, steady, reliable
- Awareness of their weaknesses or blind spots
- Willing to learn, adjust, and make changes
- Admitted mistakes; self-accountability
- Behaved ethically to the highest standards of the agency and the profession
- Excellent representative of the agency and the profession
- Written work: people were treated fairly, analysis and recommendations were without exaggeration or minimizing the facts

PROBLEM ANALYSIS

Definition: Effectively identifies problems, secures the relevant information, identifies the causes of problems, assesses the needs of employees, and evaluates for effectiveness and efficiency. Examples: performance problem, training issue, team problem, critical or tactical event, and community issue or problem.

Traits Of Lower Scoring Candidates
- Missed relevant information
- Poor listening skills
- Acted on assumptions at the expense of facts

- Missed problem issues, signs or symptoms
- Acted without having all the available information
- Jumped to pre-mature conclusions
- Inability to accept or adapt to new information
- Failed to grasp all the person's needs or agenda
- No consideration for effectiveness or efficiency
- Placed the wrong emphasis on the wrong facts
- When issues are linked, did not recognize the interrelationships or ignored the ramifications
- Focused only on superficial signs or symptoms with no effort to discover deeper issues or causes
- Little or no situational or social awareness

Traits Of Higher Scoring Candidates

- Fully identified all the problems or issues
- Effort to discover all the relevant information before deciding or acting
- Asked the right questions
- Fully assessed all the relevant needs of the person
- Identified the root causes of a problem
- Grasped all the major parts of the issue or problem
- Grasped the ramifications of the problem
- Completely assessed the impact of a decision
- Effectively interpreted laws or procedures
- Effectively used data for a reasoned analysis or identified patterns
- Effective and thorough research of an issue or problem

- Effective process to assess information and arrive at a conclusion
- When issues are linked, recognized the interrelationships
- With people, appropriate social awareness, reading non-verbal behavior, discovering other issues or agendas

JUDGMENT

Definition: Effectively develops alternative solutions to problems, evaluates courses of actions and reaches logical solutions, directs resources and people under stress, counsels employees, impartially investigates complaints, and develops strategies and objective. Examples are: critical decision making at a tactical event, a personnel issue, and prioritization of service and resources.

Traits Of Lower Scoring Candidates

- Rigid or inability to adapt to change
- Provided no alternatives to an issue or these are poorly developed without reason or facts
- Failed to show courage to do a difficult task
- Remained narrow focused at the expense of the larger picture
- Chose a course of action that was illegal, inappropriate, a poor reflection upon the agency or the profession, or was unsafe

- Acted impulsively, without thought of consequences or ramifications
- Inappropriately affected by emotion or ego
- Did not know or support the policies, practices, goals, vision, or philosophy of the agency, its leadership or the employer in public or with a subordinate
- Disclosed information that was confidential.
- Took sides without first gathering all the facts
- Used words that were profane, discriminatory, harassing, threatening, or demeaning to anyone.
- Deflected responsibility to another person inappropriately
- Failed to follow the instructions of the exercise when clearly directed.
- Little professional experience, lacks maturity

Traits Of Higher Scoring Candidates

- Adapted well to changing circumstances
- Knew what accountability is or applied it effectively
- Zeroed in on what was important
- Treated others fairly and with a just hand
- Saw the whole or bigger picture; seeing 3 or 4 steps in advance
- Forecasted and planned for events that could happen hours or days later
- Not affected by emotion or ego
- Demonstrated courage to do the difficult or hard task
- Developed sound alternatives to an issue or problem

- Effectively counseled a person and used the positive aspects of the agency's policies or practices
- Maintained confidentiality
- Was impartial in investigating a complaint
- An effective follower by fully following orders, policies or procedures
- Behaved ethically to the highest standards of the agency and the profession
- Was committed to an ethical course of action that met or exceeded the profession's standards
- Appropriately navigated through or away from emerging problems
- Has a variety of experiences to learn from

DECISIVENESS

Definition: Ready to make decisions, chooses a solution option, commits to execute a decision, reacts quickly, directs use of resources, drafts policies & procedures, establishes priorities, and responds to change. Examples are: critical decision making at a tactical event, a personnel issue, and prioritization of service and resources.

Traits Of Lower Scoring Candidates
- Did not make decisions
- Clearly ineffective while under stress
- Inappropriately unsure, uncertain, paralyzed

- Vague or unfocused
- Rigid, inflexible or unable to adapt
- Sought unnecessary assistance from supervisors
- Let others inappropriately direct or lead
- Did not own the problem; the solution or the outcome
- Passed blame or responsibility to others
- Did not identify the major technical issues that needed addressing
- Fear of taking appropriate risks
- Actions are shallow, hesitant or conditional
- Inability to be the leader, supervisor or manager
- Jumped to a premature decision without considering all the available information
- Unethical or borderline decisions or reasons

Traits Of Higher Scoring Candidates

- Demonstrated commitment to the agency's values by their work history
- Effective in making decisions under the stress of the test environment
- Decisions were clear and timely
- Reasons for the decisions were appropriate and well explained
- Acted quickly when needed or appropriate
- Showed effective and consistent command presence
- Provided leadership

- Saw the "big picture" of issues, concerns, ramifications, resources and how issues can be inter-related
- Adapted, changed when required and when supported by facts
- Knew the ramifications of a decision
- "Owned" the problem, solution and outcome
- Actions show a depth of commitment
- Identified all the technical issues that needed addressing
- Appropriate risk-taking when information is incomplete
- Strong ethical behavior
- Did not "jump" to conclusions when more information was available

PLANNING & ORGANIZING

Definition: Effectively establishes the appropriate course of action to accomplish a goal, makes assignments and uses resources appropriately; coordinates, plans, and organizes sequences; makes appropriate priorities, and effectively multi-tasks. Examples are projects, tasks, and events.

Traits Of Lower Scoring Candidates
- Inability to plan, organize and prioritize
- Micro-managed or did everything themselves
- Did the right tasks but in the wrong sequence, that was detrimental to the mission
- Inadequately recognized the goal to be accomplished

- Wrong weight on the wrong information
- Had tunnel vision with focus on only one event or task at a time
- Officious, domineering
- Did not have adequate technical knowledge of the job
- No priorities, everything had equal weight or importance
- Failed to gather relevant information or professional opinion when available
- Short-sighted
- Disorganized, impulsive, chaotic
- Uncertain, vague, waffled
- No recognition of coming issues or needs
- Failed to create trust in others
- Written: no flow of ideas, rambled, not logical, not persuasive, visually chaotic, did not meet current professional expectations

Traits Of Higher Scoring Candidates

- Effectively developed a team that accomplished a goal
- Properly assessed and used the strengths and talents of others
- Did the right tasks in the right sequence
- Able to avoid obstacles and setbacks
- Effort was both efficient and effective
- Provided effective coordination of resources
- Clearly identified the goal to be accomplished

- Communicated effectively and clearly the appropriate course of action
- Communicated appropriate values, principles or reasons to support a plan of action
- Directions and assignments were made with confidence, clarity and delivery that created respect or inspired the employee
- Effectively prioritized information
- Multi-tasked effectively with appropriate quality
- Saw the bigger picture
- Calm, focused, productive, efficient
- Correctly prioritized the importance of different factors, resources or problems
- Gathered all relevant information from best sources
- Made essential and timely notifications
- Looked ahead and recognized future needs, issues or ramifications
- Moved through setbacks
- Kept the end in-mind
- Written: clear and easy message to understand, logical, reasoned, met the current professional expectations

DELEGATION & CONTROL

Definition: Effective use of subordinates, establishes procedures to monitor and regulate activities, motivates personnel, assists others, recognizes performance problems, solves disciplinary problems, and instructs subordinates.

Traits Of Lower Scoring Candidates

- Failed to appropriately assess the needs and match up the resources needed
- Goals, objectives, mission or task were not achieved
- Did everything themselves
- Thought like a subordinate
- Failed to know what assets were available
- Made unrealistic assumptions about the capabilities that were available
- Allowed employees to be disorganized, self-deploy or self-assign tasks that is contrary to agency rules
- Failed to perceive or take action when there is chaos or disorganization
- Failed to command assets
- Used too few or too many resources on an event
- Inappropriately left employees to make preventable mistakes; no partnership or no leadership
- Failed or inadequately foresaw emerging needs of employees
- Failed to make essential and timely notifications
- Officious, controlling, or domineering
- Ineffective teaching tactics: lectured without feedback, failed to verify understanding, no display of genuine care for the employee
- Stayed in a reactive mode with no preparation for the immediate future

- No effort to monitor, verify or follow-up
- Missed essential information, clear signals or warnings

Traits Of Higher Scoring Candidates

- Goals, objectives or mission were achieved
- Knew what realistic and qualified resources were available
- Deployed resources efficiently: not too many and not too few
- Deployed resources effectively: the right staff or equipment at the right time and at the right place
- Kept the bigger picture in mind
- Motivated people by showing care for another employee, displayed loyalty and commitment
- Effectively assessed the employee's reasons for their performance
- Readily recognized employee problems
- Offered proactive assistance to employees or citizens
- Sought partnership or collaboration
- Monitored progress of events, was flexible and adjusted accordingly
- Effective teacher: created rapport and understanding of the learner through teaching, feedback, and verification of understanding
- Effective forward thinking that anticipated next steps or emerging issues before they happened
- Effort to verify or follow-up

THE KEY THEMES IN REVIEW:

- ✓ A behavioral dimension includes a number of individual characteristics and skills that an effective supervisor or manager should have.

- ✓ The assessors will be categorizing the relevant pieces of your performance into the behavioral dimensions that they are assigned to evaluate.

- ✓ Broaden your strengths into as many topics as possible. Accept the coaching that though you are strong in some areas, there are always areas that need further development. Many times, our weakness are an overuse of a strength, for example, strong listening skills can lead to the perception of being too quiet and reserved.

- ✓ If you do not effectively do or say it, you cannot receive credit for it. This is more than just content, it also how well you communicate. You could have a superior collection of experiences and training but if you cannot effectively communicate these to the assessors, the meaning may be lost. Usually, your education, training and experience is not known by the assessors and therefore it will not be given any credit in the scoring, unless you talk about it.

- ✓ Typically, the behavioral dimensions are revealed to you before the test.

- ✓ You do not have to have the best score in a behavioral dimension to be in the top tier of candidates. You need to have a consistently higher score in all of the behavioral dimensions. The most well rounded candidate that has the widest and most complete skill set and the best attitude will ultimately have the highest score.

✓ Assessors typically score three to five behavioral dimensions in each exercise. You will not know which behavioral dimensions are being scored during an exercise.

✓ For your professional development, use the "Traits of Lower Scoring Candidates" as a list of things to NOT do in your daily life and work. Use the "Traits of Higher Scoring Candidates" as a list to work on and build your set of skills and abilities.

Chapter 7

The Scoring Values & Process

T hough you have no control on scoring and the scoring process, knowing how it is done is part of the depth of understanding that will help create the shift of thinking to being the supervisor. This chapter is about the scoring values that are commonly used and includes the definitions for each value. There are different scoring processes from the individual assessor's score to the final aggregated score and we will cover the most common processes.

A test provider can use any system of scoring values for the assessors to use. The current professional practice is that the test provider should tell the candidates about the scoring system before the test. The topics to find answers to are: what is the range of values that the assessors will use, can the definitions for each value be shared with the candidate, and how is the final score arrived at?

We used the 1.0 to 5.0 point scoring model that has been advocated by the International Congress of Assessment Centers. However, one alteration was made to that model and that is eliminating the assessor's option to use the value of 1.0 as the lowest possible score for a behavioral dimension because it equates to the 20th percentile. This scoring tactic may be appropriate for the private sector but in public safety when an appropriate failing score equals the 50th percentile, if a candidate earned a 20th percentile score, should that candidate even be in the profession?

THE SCORING RANGE, VALUES AND DEFINITIONS

There are two common models of scoring values:

- 50 to 100 points. In this model, the assessors can do precision scoring in groupings of about 9 points. 100 to 90 points is Excellent, 80 to 89 points is good, 70 to 79 points is average, 60-69 points is below average, and the fixed score 55 points is not qualified.
- The more common scoring model is the 2.5 to 5.0 points model. Let's explain this model in more detail and start with the highest score possible.

5.0 Points: **Very effective and consistently excellent without any weaknesses that is clearly a step above a 4.5, and is equal to the score of 100% or the letter grade A+.**

The candidate is consistently performing at the master level for this position and can likely perform competently at the *next level higher* than the position being tested for. This candidate not only models the mastery of the essential knowledge, skills and abilities but can likely proficiently teach the required skills and abilities to others.

When you "Wow" the assessors, you could earn a 5.0. At nearly every promotional process, we saw candidates earn a 5.0. Therefore, it is possible to earn a 5.0, not by luck but by being thoroughly prepared.

4.5 Points: Very strong or excellent, and is equal to a score of 90% or the letter grade A.

The candidate's performance shows mastery of most of the core performance expectations and exceeds most of the expectations of the behavioral dimension. Their knowledge, skills, abilities, style and execution of the dimension is fully formed, polished and has depth. They can easily adapt their skills and abilities to new situations with ease and effectiveness. The candidate is performing at or near the master level.

Typically, the specific expectations that are provided to the assessors are crafted or approved by the subject matter expert are written to this 4.5 level. These expectations are often in bullet point format and are in front of the assessors during your performance. Therefore, when you see the assessors checking boxes as you go through the exercise that is a good thing! This is your main target score.

4.0 Points: More than adequate and minimally competent and is equal to a score of 80% or the letter grade B.

The candidate's performance exceeds most of the performance expectations of the position being tested for. They are effective at not only the core tasks of the job but also at many of the minor ones. Their style is becoming polished and their delivery or execution of the dimension shows a depth of confidence and it is closely aligned with the agency's and profession's mission, values or principles. The candidate has room for improvement to perform at the master level and is essentially performing at the journeyman level.

This is that middle ground between Excellent and Average. To be a top candidate, this is the minimum score you need.

3.5 Points: **Minimally adequate and competent for a *newly promoted supervisor*, and equal to a score of 70% or the letter grade C.**

The candidate's performance meets all the minimum expectations of the dimension for a newly promoted supervisor or manager. The candidate is ready for promotion without the need for substantial additional time or training to perform the **core tasks** of the job effectively and consistently.

However, supervision, training and experience are necessary for the candidate to continue to hone skills, achieve an effective style, rise to the journeyman level and grow into the complexities of the position. When taken as a whole, the candidate is at the student level of being a supervisor. This score is the equivalent to the test process' minimum passing score.

3.0 Points: **Nearly competent or adequate, equal to a score of 60% or the letter grade D.**

The candidate's performance is not consistently competent in all the core areas or minimum expectations of the dimension and therefore the candidate is not yet ready for promotion to the position. More experience, knowledge, training and supervision are appropriate for the candidate to perform the core tasks of the position.

2.5 Points: **Substantially below adequate, and equal to a score of 50%, or the letter grade F.**

The candidate's performance was substantially problematic or it does not consistently meet most of the major expectations of the job, most of the time. A candidate who earned this score is highly likely to not being capable of performing adequately if promoted, and their performance is likely to be consistently substandard and problematic, even with direct supervision at the time of their promotion.

What causes one candidate to earn a 3.5 and another candidate to earn a 4.5 in the same dimension? The answer is complicated because a behavioral dimension includes many characteristics. The main difference is the 4.5-scoring candidate clearly nailed all the specific expectations for the exercise AND met the "Traits Of Higher Scoring Candidates" that are listed in the Scoring Guidelines in the previous chapter.

Here are two important key themes:

Key Theme: Higher scoring candidates possess more wisdom, are more fully formed and seasoned, have a wide and deep skill set, are confident and comfortable "in their own skin" and demonstrate the passion or enthusiasm for the position. Top candidates love their agency and are thoroughly committed to the ideals and values of the profession.

Key Theme: Work on your whole spectrum of skills and abilities, balancing and developing the depth of your skill set and strengthening the weaker areas.

How do you do this? By continual improvement through self-study, education, experience and training. Without the proper self-assessment of your skills and abilities and the desire to re-invent yourself through a committed and sustained effort, you may be outcompeted by those who do. More on this in Chapter 10.

THE SCORING PROCESS

Earning an empirical score for each dimension is one of the best practices in building an assessment center. A process that involve the assessors only ranking the candidates through a voting process is a weak process because it is not objective or defensible. Scoring that is not supported by the documenting of objective evidence is a flawed process.

The scoring begins when either the assessors finish their introduction of the exercise and start the timer or when you enter the exercise room and a role-player is present. Scoring continues through the job simulation and your response to questions and stops when you leave the exercise room.

SCORING PROCESS MODELS

Test providers use several different scoring models. Though you will not be able to choose or influence the model that your process will have, if you understand each model you can be mentally better prepared by being more at ease with what is happening. This leads to being more focused and showing the depth of your traits to be the next supervisor or manager. Let's talk about the different scoring models:

1. Consensus Scoring. After you leave the exercise, each assessor will engage in two phases of scoring. In Phase 1, the assessor will privately assign a score value for each behavioral dimension using one of the stated scoring values that was described above. In Phase 2, the panel of assessors will agree upon a consensus score for each behavioral dimension, using 1/100th of a point that can be within the range of values between the lowest Phase 1 score and 5.0, the highest value. Assessors may be told that candidates cannot receive the same score for the same behavioral dimension because this creates more separation between the candidates.

   An example of this scoring process is one assessor gives a score of 4.0 and the other assessor gives 4.5 and after a discussion, they arrive at a consensus score of 4.15. The working definition of consensus is, "I may not totally agree, but I can live with it."

   The strength of this model is the sharing of information and the deliberation and negotiation between the assessors of what is important for every behavioral dimension. Assessors see and hear different things and place an emphasis on different traits. A consensus score is often better supported with more objective evidence. The weakness of this model is that consensus takes time and effort and this can impact the schedule for the entire test day by limiting the number of candidates that the assessors can evaluate. This model is generally hard to do with very large groups of candidates because of the time required.

2. Value Averaging. After the exercise each assessor makes a private score for each of the behavioral dimensions. Some test providers allow the assessors to share their impressions of the candidate before scoring but the actual point value is not discussed. Assessors can score to the $1/10^{th}$ of a point. Some test providers add an additional step called "forced scoring" meaning that every assessor must be within one point of each other. These scores immediately leave the assessors and the scores for the same behavioral dimension are averaged together.

   The weaknesses of this model: there is little to no sharing or negotiation of impressions and that if there are only two assessors and one score is dramatically lower than the other, getting the assessors to be only 1 point a part may not be defensible. To mitigate this weakness, a minimum of three assessors are needed and more is better.

3. Exercise Scoring. After you leave, each assessor assigns a score for each behavioral dimension. Then, for each assessor, all of the dimensions are added together. The scores from each assessor are added together to create your final score for the exercise.

   In this model, each exercise is a stand-alone test and there is a minimum score for each exercise. In this model, the individual behavioral dimension is not as important as in the other models. The weaknesses of this model are: The assessors in one exercise can have more power over the final outcome by being able inflate scores and if a candidate fails one exercise, they fail the promotional test. This model is common in the fire service but is falling out of favor because of the frequency of challenges.

Key Theme: During an exercise, do not dwell on the perception that an assessor is giving you negative feedback. First, the assessor may be concentrating on recording their observations and their non-verbal message is not intentional. Second, an individual assessor's raw and individual score often does not move forward in the scoring process. Plus, in dimensional scoring with a small set of behavioral dimensions, different assessors score each behavioral dimension at least twice; in different exercises and therefore, one panel's scores in one dimension does not have a major affect on your overall score.

The employer decides the scoring model when the test provider is hired. Your employer should tell you which model is being used before the promotional test.

WEIGHTING THE BEHAVIORAL DIMENSIONS

Weighting is about identifying that a particular behavioral dimension or exercise is more important than the others. Weighting is an option that many clients like because it is an empirical method to better reflect the agency's desired skill set for the future supervisor or manager. Weighting also reflects the unique personality of the agency. For example, one agency may place a higher value on a candidate's judgment, while another agency's priority may be interpersonal insight.

The personnel rules, collective bargaining agreement or policy will often state if weighting is permitted or not. If the rules are silent on this topic, it may be allowed and some rules are quite detailed in how the weighting is done. Most of the time, the rules are silent and the employer works with the test provider on creating a weighting process.

The weight factor often has a significant impact on scoring the candidates who are in the middle of the list. Typically, the weight factor will not impact the top candidates or the bottom ones because their scores are high or low. It will often re-order the middle tier of candidates.

Of all the behavioral dimensions, those involving Judgment are almost always the most weighted. The second most weighted behavioral dimension is Interpersonal Insight. For the position of Sergeant, the least valued behavioral dimension is usually Planning and Organization. For the command positions, the behavioral dimensions of Decisiveness and Writing will share the top weighted dimensions.

Key Theme: Put more emphasis on developing your skills of Judgment and Interpersonal Insight. See the scoring guidelines for these two behavioral dimensions on pages 78 and 74 for more specific information on what higher scoring candidates do.

Because the weight factor can impact the scoring, the leadership team is sometimes surprised about the list of candidates. This often happens when their favorite candidate has superior skills in one behavioral dimension that is not the most highly valued behavioral dimension. We have frequently seen candidates with superior oral communication skills and are favored by the leadership team, but when they earn average scores in Judgment, they end up in the middle of the list. Typically, the favored candidate has a high "like-ability index" meaning most people just like the candidate and this often causes the leadership team to pause when the scores are revealed. This is another reason why a well-constructed assessment center is valid, objective and defensible.

Usually, the weight factor is determined by the completion of a survey by the agency's managers and executives. The best practices are that the assessors and the candidates are not told what the weight factor is to keep the playing field level with all the candidates. Also, the agency's leadership team usually does not know the results of the surveys, so they cannot construct the exercises to favor a specific candidate's skills.

OTHER TOPICS AND FAQ'S ABOUT SCORING

Do role players score?

Answer: Typically, no for several reasons: (1) they may not be qualified assessors, and (2) it is difficult to be an actor and an evaluator of the whole dynamic at the same time because they will miss information. However, the input from role players may be welcome by the assessors as they do their deliberations.

Can assessors change their score when they start comparing candidates?

Answer: Depends on the structure of the scoring process made by the test provider. Sometimes the answer is no, especially when Value Averaging is used and the scores are picked up from the assessors immediately. Some test providers will leave the score sheets with the assessors for the whole test day and encourage the assessors to continually rank order the candidates.

Is testing at a specific part of the test day more advantageous?

Answer: There is no good way to answer that because there is little data available. We know that from using the Consensus Model and leaving the scoresheets with the assessors who have the photographs of all the candidates, there is no evidence that a morning candidate or the last candidate did better.

What if an assessor not only knows me but we have horrible history and I am certain that I cannot be assessed fairly?

Answer: Ask the test provider about this before the test and call their attention to it immediately after the exercise. The test provider should be able to describe their planned strategy for this event. Because we did Consensus Scoring that had two phases of documented scoring, we could tell when an assessor had a dramatic influence on the other assessor and action could be taken afterwards.

After the exercises and the scoring, there is often a debrief of the assessors. What happens and can the leadership team change the scoring?

Answer: Most test providers conduct a debrief of the assessors and many times, the personnel rules allow the leadership team to witness their impressions. They listen but cannot join the discussion or challenge the assessors to support their score. The value for the leadership team to hear the debrief includes new information about candidates, the impact of their leadership on the candidates, and trends within the agency. The best practices include scoring that is finalized before the debrief and no one can change the numbers.

After the scoring is finished, what happens next?

Answer: The scores are given to the employer who will add other testing components such as a written test, a work performance rating, credits for military service and years of service. These credits are described in the employer's personnel rules. Many rules describe an appeal period for candidate's to challenge the test. Sometimes the scores are released after the appeal period and sometimes before. Again, all of this is described in your employer's rules.

THE SCORE SHEET

Typically, the assessor's score sheet is the only work product left at the end of the testing process because it is intended to be a stand-alone document. Like the notes made by the candidates, the assessor's notes are destroyed at the end of the test day. Why? Because the notes do not contain all of the information that supports an assessor's score and can create preventable confusion weeks or months after the test.

Test providers design their score sheets differently. Often, the score sheet has three parts: (1) the numbers: the assessor's individual score for each behavioral dimension and the panel's consensus score for each behavioral dimension, (2) a description of the candidate's actions and words that support the assessor's score, and (3) the assessor's subjective comments that are intended to be a message to the candidate and those are described below.

Whether you will be able to see the assessor's score sheet after the test is determined by the rules of your agency. Typically, test providers do not release scores, information or documents to the candidates because the test provider is working for the agency not the candidate. Scores are released by your employer using their personnel or civil service rules.

COMMENDATIONS AND RECOMMENDATIONS

The bulk of the score sheet is the recording of objective facts and the assignment of scores. A good practice by test providers is to have the assessors also make <u>subjective comments</u> that are intended to be direct messages to candidates that highlight the commendations of their performance and recommendations for improvement. These should be taken in the spirit that they were created, to help direct a personal quest for improvement. These comments are not part of the final score; they are only the gift of feedback from the assessors to the candidates.

Here are **samples of commendations and recommendations** that were given to other candidates and may be of value in your preparation. Note that some of the comments are behaviors to *emulate* and others are ones to *avoid*.

- Good job identifying the key problem issues with reports; recognized substandard performance;
- Displayed calm confident demeanor with good use of verbal skills; strong introduction that quickly diffused the angry citizen;
- Improve your knowledge of criminal procedures to avoid making poor decisions on search and seizure

issues; think "big picture" and don't spend time on details that are not necessary

- Be sure to include all the problem areas and address the actions to be taken; conclude the memo with a strong closing;

- Very professional communication with irate citizen; offered a variety of solutions and was patient and thorough in diffusing the situation and determining what the real issues were;

- Knew the department policies well, put victims first, and decisions were made in the proper order with thought to the consequences;

- Develop the differences between being a teacher and a supervisor when addressing performance issues; practice one to one face time which may be outside your comfort zone;

- Direct the conversation better and don't be too thorough and detailed; focus on what solves the citizen's problem not necessarily the holistic situation at this time;

- Consider the big picture but be aware of time issues as competing events are happening simultaneously; delegate responsibility to the officers on the scene; don't become directly involved in every event;

- Be sure to establish timelines, goals, expectations, and consequences of an officer's behavior;

- Outstanding command presence and provided great suggestions to solve the issues; saw the "big picture" with problem reports; showed true leadership;

- Get involved with younger or less experienced employees and offer to help mentor them; look for more opportunities to practice already well developed leadership potential;

- Don't let the citizen "drive the train" and be more organized in developing and explaining the problem-solving plan;

- The media will not go away, so use your resources (such as the Public Information Officer) to help when busy;

- Be sure to discuss the consequences of failing to improve or continued poor performance with the employee;

- Proof read your reports to address spelling, grammar, and punctuation errors; include corrective action, goals, and timelines; don't push the issues up to the commander for a decision; make your recommendations;

- Good use of verbal interpersonal skills to diffuse the situation to solve the problem to the complainant's satisfaction; asked clarifying questions and had good suggestions for alternatives with commitment for specific follow-up;

- Learn to manage multiple events from a supervisory perspective with finite resources; practice keeping track of resources so that all events are handled; let others handle the work as your job as supervisor is to ensure the work gets done, not do it yourself;

- Have a clear plan of what you want to communicate and be sure to schedule a follow-up meeting;

- Calm and comfortable during presentation with good use of time management;

- Able to recognize first priorities during critical events and was insightful and thoughtful in making decisions;

- Articulate, clear and direct communication with a good introduction that laid out the reason for the meeting; showed what was expected with a follow-up plan;

- Be more assured/assertive with command presence and take responsibility as a supervisor for the issues directly, as opposed to having a FTO work with an officer;

- Have a specific plan in mind so you are able to immediately take control of the citizen's complaint and don't treat the situation like a witness statement;

- Learn to supervise multiple events from a supervisor perspective, seeing the "big picture" when assigning and prioritizing resources and keeping track of assets available; don't treat each event individually but as part of a whole;

- Good basic knowledge of standards of reports and issues and solutions for addressing problems;

- Good ability to diffuse the angry citizen and being polite;

- Ideas in the memo were broken into easy to read paragraphs; identified three issues in need of correction and good use of quotes;

- Take full advantage of the presentation during an exercise to confidently explain and present your thinking and solutions;
- Slow down your speech; listen carefully to fully understand the problem; take ownership of the problem and offer solutions and follow up;
- Good initiative on tasks and expectations;
- Verified information with citizen and listened with empathy;
- Sense of easy demeanor and rapport yet also command presence during officer counseling;
- Balanced reassuring statements that also highlighted seriousness of the issue;
- Took command and delegated appropriately with a smooth delivery and good command presence;
- Good analysis of arrest sequence with good overview toward possible contingencies;
- Read instructions carefully for details, time, and priorities; assign a specific officer to complete a resource plan;
- Don't assume an employee is guilty just from a complaint;
- Great leadership development and demonstration of core values when using the Field Training Officer comparison during officer counseling;
- Articulate explanations and all errors were found with thorough follow-up of reports;

- Practice public speaking and work on a fluid and organized delivery;
- Never tell a citizen that you have reviewed information when you have not;
- Good control of conversation with citizen; deescalated frustration; self-confident and saw the big picture;
- In-basket: Start with top priority and then move to lower ones;
- Develop rapport before discussing discipline. Slow down and have a conversation with the officer;
- Avoid minimizing verbal reprimand;
- Very good job with decision-making and explanations of in-basket;
- Do not commit to a course of action until you have talked to the employee about the complaint;
- Present the agency's values and "principle tenets;"
- Good language and facial expressions that showed care & concern; cool and professional during counseling;
- Could have empathized more and recognized the citizen's frustrations;
- Work on a rapport/discipline mode rather than an investigative mode when counseling;
- Don't rely too heavily on an investigative approach to critical events; think more first responder/initial response;
- Well spoken, kept citizen on track and was persuasive and articulate with the issues;

- Used humor in an appropriate way while bridging to the seriousness of the issue;
- An easy demeanor but still kept a strong command presence;
- Good details and sequencing of plans during critical events especially in locating the vehicle;
- Practice thinking like a supervisor when reviewing reports; include necessary follow-up and training;
- Strong in initiative and motivation, as well as tactical decisions and delegation;
- Good job slowing down the critical event situation;
- Practice multi-dimensional thinking and managing priorities that is required of a supervisor;
- Conveyed genuine concern for why the employee had lost her cool;
- Be more assertive, make decisions, and be more specific on how to handle supervisor issues;
- Study the discipline structure of your organization and present specific solutions if you identify stressors with an employee;
- Worked hard on building consensus and offering solutions to citizen; calm yet in control and verified facts and information; and
- Smooth deployment of resources in an orderly manner with detailed contingencies planned during critical events.

THE KEY THEMES IN REVIEW:

- ✓ Higher scoring candidates possess more wisdom, are more fully formed and seasoned, have a wide and deep skill set, are confident and comfortable "in their own skin" and demonstrate the passion or enthusiasm for the position.

- ✓ Top candidates love their agency and are thoroughly committed to the ideals and values of the profession.

- ✓ Work on balancing and developing the depth of your skill set and strengthening the weaker areas because the top tier candidates are strong in many areas.

- ✓ Use the position's Job Description to discover the core duties and work at developing more than a student level of expertise.

- ✓ During an exercise, do not dwell on the perception that an assessor is giving you negative feedback.

- ✓ Depending upon the scoring model, you can do poorly in one exercise and still pass an assessment center because there are many scores created and the weight factor added in the final scoring process is often a driver. Marginal candidates will let their perception of their performance in one exercise affect the performance in other exercises.

✓ Put more emphasis on developing your skills of Judgment and Interpersonal Insight. See the scoring guidelines for these two behavioral dimensions.

✓ Study the lessons told to other candidates that are in the form of commendations and recommendations for coaching and guidance.

Chapter 8

Types Of Exercises And Keys For Success

Your agency will chose a variety of exercises or job simulations that are intended to capture a range of the major duties that the position does in the organization. For clarity in this chapter, the terms exercises and job simulations mean the same thing: a planned and structured event where you respond to a set of information, are the supervisor or manager, and are assessed on what you say and do in that role. Essentially if you have made the transition to thinking like a supervisor, you will do better.

The kinds of exercises that are commonly used in a promotional process are:

- Counseling or teaching an employee,
- Meeting with a citizen or customer of the agency to resolve a concern,

- Making an oral presentation to managers, employees or citizens that simulates a meeting, a briefing, or public presentation,

- Analyzing information, assessing possible solutions and making a recommendation to a decision maker,

- Dealing with a number of topics, issues or information that have a range of different priorities and includes making decisions, taking action, and delegating tasks to others,

- Tactical or critical thinking – decision making job simulations that are potential real-life situations that could occur in the community and inside the organization, and

- Writing exercises.

You can find information on the Internet and in other books about exercises done at assessment centers. However, a word of caution on using these to prepare: There are lots of sources to explain exercises and provide answers and solutions. Use these sources to expand your thinking and to develop your skill set but do not be rigid that these will be used at your test process and be skeptical that the suggestions or answers are the best answer; simply do not memorized someone else's answer.

Key Theme: Do not memorize someone else's answer or solution as it (1) may be wrong for your agency's exercise and expectations and (2) it will not sound authentic or genuine, which could result in a lower score.

As a reminder, every exercise has a specific set of expectations of what a strong and higher scoring candidate should be able to do. Your agency's subject matter expert created or approved these expectations. Therefore, the assessors have these expectations and the scoring guidelines for each behavioral dimension to guide them in their scoring. Without these specific expectations, the assessors will bring their own expectations from their agency and environment, and this will erode the validity of the promotional test.

Let's talk about the common exercises that are often given to an agency to choose from. The exercise will be described, keys to success will be listed and additional information to help you in your preparation will be offered.

STRUCTURED INTERVIEW

The structured interview is still the most common part of promotional testing. It is a tradition of clients, candidates expect it and assessors love it. Many times, the highest scores come from the structured interview and most candidates do well with a narrow band of scores between the highest and lowest candidate. However, it is not a job simulation and does not involve a role player.

For a 20 to 30 minute time with the assessors, you can expect about 8 to 10 questions. We recommend to clients that the questions be given to you in the prep area. Why are these given ahead of time? Because these questions are designed to be complex, about in-depth topics and with no simple right or wrong answer. Your answers are intended to reveal your experience, skills, values, character, and knowledge.

When a candidate is surprised by a question, their answer is often shallow, disorganized, key parts are often missed and the candidate who verbalizes well will often throw a lot of thoughts on the wall and see what sticks. Rather than the test measuring the candidate's wisdom and character, it measures their ability to remember the question. When these questions are provided 10 to 15 minutes before the exercise, the candidate's answers are richer, deeper and will better reflect their attributes. Because this is not a memorization exercise, you should be able to take the questions and your notes from the prep area into the exercise room.

When a structured interview is not chosen by an agency as a stand-alone exercise, other exercises are often concluded with two or three interview-style questions that are generally relevant to the exercise. This is intended to give you another "bite at the apple" at displaying your abilities and these questions are also provided in the prep area. For example, the exercise is coaching an employee about a minor performance issue. After the role player leaves the exercise room, the assessors ask, "Tell us about a time that you had to coach an employee or co-worker and they improved. Also, tell us what lessons you learned from this experience."

Often, the structured interview exercise will start with a question that will give you the opportunity to provide a brief summation of your qualifications for the position. This is a softball question that you should be able to hit over the fence because it is about the subject you know most about: you.

Top candidates will answer the oral resume question with a listing of their **most important** knowledge, skills and abilities, in priority order that is <u>specifically relevant to the position</u>. They will keep the list confined to the major themes of supervision and leadership and will provide supporting evidence. However, they balance this with sufficient detail that sends the message that they are truly prepared for the promotion. Marginal candidates will do a chronological narrative from birth to the present and list all the schools and training that they attended, which is generally boring, not memorable and results in lower scores.

Typically, this "tell us about you" question may include a time element, such as, "In about two minutes" or "In 90 seconds what are the most important things that we should know about you?" This means that your answer should be brief and succinct and the content is the most important information. The assessors may or may not be timing this question. If they are, you will see them start a timer and they will stop the narrative when time has elapsed.

This kind of question may also be at the end of an exercise, such as, "What else should we know about you, that is really important?" Questions like these are opportunities to provide some history about you that is unavailable to the assessors. After all, they typically do not have your application or your resume and by design, can only score you on what you say and do in the exercise room.

We end this topic of the oral resume with two key themes:

Key Theme: Use the preparation for your oral resume as the cornerstone of your foundation to transition to thinking like a supervisor. Select the experiences that changed you and inspired you to move into leadership. Delve deeply into your skill set and abilities and seek out the areas of knowledge and skills that are lacking and use that awareness as a motivation to learn. Clarify your thinking about why you want to be a supervisor.

Key Theme: Decide in advance the high-level message or personal theme that you want the assessors to learn about you and practice that message so it is effective.

TYPES OF INTERVIEW QUESTIONS

The **types of questions** that are commonly used in interviews are: Conceptual, Specific Issue, Personal Insight and Experiential. Let's describe each of these.

CONCEPTUAL questions require creating a unique answer that **is personal and from your perspective** rather than recalling, and reciting prior knowledge. There are no right or wrong answers, just well developed answers or not so developed. The top tier answers are a blend of well-articulated values and principles that are heart-felt with the application of technical knowledge that pertains to the subject.

The KEYS TO SUCCESS are:

- Great answers will show your personal insight, the depth of your self-awareness and your willingness to be honest about yourself.

- Appropriately tying in the agency's mission and values and the core ideals of the profession can be effective, providing that you are sincere and genuine.

Examples of a Conceptual Question are:

a) As a new supervisor (or manager), what steps will you take within your first 90 days to establish goals and expectations for your team?

b) Describe your supervisory style. How would you ensure that your employees and your fellow supervisors would work together to be consistent with adherence to policies, procedures, and rules?

c) What do you think the command staff should do more of and what should the command staff do less of?

d) Where will you draw the line between what you offer to share with your boss and what you don't share regarding the behavior and performance of your people?

e) The phrase, "You deserve the performance that you tolerate" is one of the core parts of supervising people. What does this mean to you?

The pitfalls to avoid are to make stuff up, be vague, not answer the question on point, and be hesitant about revealing yourself. Other mistakes to avoid are to be critical of others, be negative or use the question as a confession of your personal wounded-ness. There is an appropriate time and place for these, but the promotional test is not one of them.

SPECIFIC ISSUE questions are about topics that are relevant to your agency. They can come from the past, present or future. These issues are typically consuming some organizational energy and often have one thing in common: the topic is about adapting to change.

The KEYS TO SUCCESS are:

- Create a list of your agency's current challenges, issues, and the coming programs or changes. Add to this list a description of your depth of knowledge of these and your views of them. Then work on your gaps of knowledge and learn what the leadership team's approaches to these are.

Examples of Specific Issue questions are:

a) Why is a system of accountability and discipline important for an organization and whose responsibility is it for maintaining discipline?

b) Transparency and responsiveness are strategies for earning the public's trust. Describe what you can do in this position to further these?

c) Name two projects or programs that your agency needs to implement. Tell us why you feel these would benefit your agency and the community.

d) What will you do to get the most out of your subordinates and what will you do for those who are not performing to your expectations?

e) Handling calls relating to homelessness and drug addiction is causing much frustration with your subordinates. They are complaining about lack of resources, problems that do not go away and high expectations of the community. What can you do as the supervisor to create a higher morale and sense of satisfaction?

The pitfalls to avoid are to be not prepared with knowing what the possible issues could be and to not have thought about what you would do and the reasons behind your answer.

Many specific issue questions are related to the topic of how leadership is carried out. All of these questions can be partially answered by communicating these themes of leadership:

- Lead by example,
- Model a positive answer,
- Set specific, attainable and time-limited expectations,
- Deal with performance issues quickly,
- Be the balance of an advocate and holding people accountable,
- Share as much information as possible,
- If you do not care about the people you lead, you do not deserve to lead them, and
- That many times the best solution is in the minds of those who are going to do the work.

PERSONAL INSIGHT questions are intended to reveal your wisdom, maturity, character, knowledge and emotional intelligence.

The KEYS TO SUCCESS are:

- Genuine answers that reveal both confidence and uncertainty,
- Demonstrate that learning is a lifestyle, not an event.
- Dig deep to be aware of your strengths and weaknesses

Examples of Personal Insight questions are:

a) If we talked to the employees under your command (or your co-workers) who liked you the least, what would they say are your shortcomings?

b) The best candidates have a full compliment of experience, knowledge, skills and abilities. If you are promoted, which of these is the one that you will rely upon the most and which is the one that you will need to build?

c) Everyone has made a mistake that had consequences or ramifications that affected other people. What did you learn from a mistake that you made?

d) Explain how you have prepared yourself to be a leader in this agency and specifically what have you done to shore up your weaknesses?

e) If you are not promoted how will you overcome your disappointment and what steps will you take to prepare for the next promotional process?

EXPERIENTIAL questions are intended to draw out your experience in a specific area. Rather than an academic or hypothetical response, the answer comes from your prior work performance. Of all the categories of questions, this is the one that **most** clients **choose most** of the questions from. Experiential questions typically begin with these words, "Tell us about a time when . . . ." or "Give us an example of . . . ." and the rest of question is often from one of these areas:

- ✓ Guide or coach an employee,
- ✓ Motivate an employee,
- ✓ Deal with a difficult employee,
- ✓ Deal with a difficult citizen,
- ✓ Decision making in a critical or tactical event,
- ✓ Make an unpopular decision,

✓ Deal with an employee who is making negative and untrue remarks about another employee or the leadership team,

✓ Need to support a decision, policy or procedure that is unpopular,

✓ Take the initiative and provide leadership

The KEYS TO SUCCESS are:

- Choose an experience from your history that reflects the **best of your abilities** rather than the one that was the most recent or had the most impact on you. The assessors are gathering evidence that you provide them, so give them the best possible.

- Using a compelling example that directly answers the question will earn more points.

- Tell the story well but within the time constraints. The story must include the context of the situation. So set the stage with the environment and what was at stake.

- Whether or not the question asks for it, try to incorporate into every answer **what you learned from the experience**. This self-awareness will elevate you above the candidates who do not offer it.

You can probably see that effectively answering experiential questions is tricky and that is why preparation is so important. What if you do not have an experience at work, what are your options? You can use a non-work experience but keep it relevant to the question and emphasize the lessons you learned. What if you have no experience at all about the topic? Then, tell the assessors, "I have no direct experience with that topic but this is what I would do . . . . ." and give a thorough answer that demonstrates your depth of knowledge. The notion here is that a satisfactory answer is better than no answer. Do your preparation by doing your own inventory from your experiences and then select the best events for this promotional process.

Examples of Experiential questions are:

a) Tell us about a time that you successfully provided guidance or coaching to a co-worker that resulted in them doing a better a job.

b) Tell us about a time that you saw a co-worker do or say something that was contrary to the agency's policy or practices and you did something about it.

c) Give us an example of a time when you had to conform to a policy with which you did not agree. What was the outcome and what did your learn from it?

d) Give us an example of how you model ethics and integrity.

e) Effective leaders are innovative and proactive. Tell us two things you have done to demonstrate these qualities.

CONCLUSION QUESTIONS. Typically, interview exercises end with a final question, "Is there anything else that you would like to add or change to any previous answer?" This question opens a large door of opportunity for the candidate because it contains two separate parts in one question. One, are there changes to a previous answer including adding anything new? Two, is there anything else that you would like to add? Like many questions in a promotional test, when you read the question slowly, the nuances, parts and complexities of the question become apparent.

The intention is to give you one final opportunity to give evidence to the assessors that you are ready for this promotion. The marginal candidate will fail to grasp this opportunity and is probably focused on getting out of the room and they will quickly say, "No, I'm good."

The KEYS TO SUCCESS are:

- Prepare for the opportunity of providing additional information to an answer by deciding that you will take three seconds to think about it. When the assessors see that you are pausing and thinking, the message is received that you are thoughtful and deliberate.

- If you know that you under talked or rambled on with an answer, an effective tactic is to own this with the assessors. For example, "I was really too brief on what I would do to coach an employee, here are three things that I want to emphasize." Or, "Reflecting about how to deal with a difficult morale problem, I think I was too vague. So, let me be quite specific with this point . . . ."

- Seize the opportunity to summarize in a quick sound bite or a bold headline the final message that you want the assessors to know about you.

- Walk through the door that the assessors are holding open for you when asked, "Is there anything else?"

- How an interview starts and how it ends is remembered the most.

What is your final message? A great topic is one that the

assessors are desperate waiting for: **Why** do you want this job and why should you be promoted? Answer this question in a personal and heartfelt way. If you sincerely believe in the ideals of the profession: service, making a difference, leaving a situation better than you found it, duty, honor, and helping the vulnerable and those who are hurting, then weave these into your answer. If you have embraced your agency's values and mission, then say so and explain why being promoted is part of your personal journey.

You can do a lot of repair work by having a spectacular conclusion of no longer than 90 seconds. This is not something that is made up in the moment, it is a finely honed message that begins with digging deep inside you, brainstorming and considering a number of messages and themes and then honing it down to a clear and concise message that is etched on your heart and delivered with passion.

The KEYS TO SUCCESS FOR ANSWERING ALL QUESTIONS are:

1. <u>Know your message before answering.</u> Taking a moment to gather your thoughts is perfectly acceptable. Rehearse what three seconds feels like. In that time, thoughts can be sorted and perfected. For the assessors, three seconds is very comfortable and 10 seconds is too long. Have a clear purpose because without one, it is like a trip without a destination. Be thoughtful and deliberate and know where you are going with the answer. Stop yourself from meandering or babbling. When in doubt or if the assessors act disinterested, simply stop talking and after a pause say, "I am ready for the next question."

2. <u>Show your ownership of the agency</u> and the profession with expressions like, "This is my team." "Your problem is now my problem." "This problem was important to solve because I care about these people, this is my community."

3. <u>Monitor your communication style.</u> Remember the words you choose or the text of your answer is only a part of the message. Effectively use all the non-verbal strategies: eye contact, sitting up straight, appropriate gestures, conveys a positive message. Project confidence with clear diction and avoid fading out at the end of sentences. Maintain a momentum and a cadence with a range of voice volume and speed in your narrative. Your answer should sound interesting. We cannot help but love good storytelling. Think about how good stories are told and practice your speaking.

4. <u>Engage with the assessors.</u> Make eye contact with all the assessors; show your enthusiasm and passion for the job and your loyalty to the agency. Do this by scanning the entire panel of assessors, back and forth. Avoid addressing only one assessor and ignoring the others. Be willing to show your true self because that will separate you from the candidates who are working hard to act, pretend, and say what they think the assessors want to hear.

5. <u>Show courtesy, gratitude and command presence.</u> Begin and end the interview with a sincere expression of

gratitude to the assessors for participating in this important process. A sincere smile is the shortest distance between two people and an authentic and meaningful handshake will create a lasting impression.

6. <u>Be wary of distracting verbal and non-verbal behavior or habits.</u> All of us can have distracting mannerisms and the damage can be huge. A well-crafted message will be ignored or forgotten. A distracting verbal habit is using filler words like, OK, Ah, Um and the over use of words, for example, "like." All of these become distractors when the assessors start counting how many times they are used. How do you know you have one? Record yourself and you will discover the gap between what you think you do and what you really do. Narrowing the gap through self-awareness is the goal. Examples of a distracting non-verbal behavior are rapidly clicking the ballpoint pen, swiveling around in the chair, shaking the car keys in the pants pocket, covering the mouth while talking, and sucking candy while talking.

7. <u>Using humor</u> is a double-edged sword; it can be very effective but it can also hurt you. Well-done humor is relaxing for everyone, shows you are a multi-faceted person and are personable. The safest topic for humor is you. Poking a little fun at your weaknesses or fears can be appropriate. Avoid humor that is selective to a certain person, gender, race or class, or is demeaning or profane. A great interview will be quickly spoiled by one mistake.

8. <u>Watch your time,</u> in a good way rather than in a restrictive way. Pace yourself to fully answer a question but do not rob yourself of the opportunity to answer the others. There are two mistakes to avoid by the candidate who failed to manage their time: being long-winded and is stopped by the assessors because time has run out and being so concerned about time that they answer so briefly or speak extremely fast and leave a substantial amount of time on the table.

9. <u>Be genuine in speaking about others</u> in a positive way and be loyal to the leadership team. If you are not genuine, the assessors will pick up on this deceptive behavior and act accordingly with lower scores. Do not throw others under the bus and do not make the interview a confessional where your sins are aired.

    Show humility by not being a braggart who takes credit. Over-using the word "I" is a trap to avoid because you will sound arrogant, selfish and self-centered.

    Several themes of leadership to consider including in your presentation are: standing beside employees as a way to assist them, developing employees by sharing information, giving employees opportunities to lead, and removing the noise or obstacles that can get in the way of a great performance.

10. <u>Grow your reputation and credibility.</u> View your credibility as a savings account. Every positive act of recognizing, guiding, supporting, helping and encouraging others is a deposit into your credibility

account. When you make a mistake or have to make a difficult or unpopular decision, there is a withdrawal from your account. The key is to keep a positive balance.

Do not be a BMW (bitcher, moaner and whiner) as they are rarely chosen by the management team to lead. Discover what your reputation is early in your preparation by asking people who will be honest with you. If they describe you as being overly critical, skeptical, cynical, a pessimist or a soloist who does not work well with others, those may be coded words that you are a BMW.

The only fix is to immediately stop cold turkey and work to be a convert who is positive, committed and loyal to the principles and ethics of the profession. Not surprisingly, these are the peers that we truly like to be around. Your professional reputation is one of the few things you have control over and either it will open doors for you or it will limit your opportunities. You own your reputation by your outward actions but it is carried and delivered by others who speak about you. Your reputation is slow to grow and fast and easy to lose.

11. <u>Tell a story that is truthful, compelling and is supported with examples from your experience</u>. Consider using a way to tell your story that makes sense to the assessors, such as the acronym **SAR** that stands for **S**ituation, **A**ction and **R**esponse. The *situation* describes the context, such as, "I was working swing shift with five other employees and I was training a new employee." *Action* describes the core problem or opportunity, such as "We handled an accident scene where the new employee planned an unsafe way to

move traffic." *Response* describes how the problem or issue was resolved and how the participants responded to your actions, such as, "I showed the new employee how to place the vehicles and cones to make a safe and effective lane for traffic."

A story sandwich is another way to organize your narrative: tell them what you are going to talk about, tell them the story, then finish with a summary of what you told them.

12. <u>Respect your audience.</u> If you have military experience, do not ignore it or minimize it. But, know your audience. Non-military assessors will not understand the unique language of terms or the environment of your service. Explain the setting, the mission, how many employees you supervised and the length and complexity of the assignment.

Also, many candidates who come from the military will not give detailed answers and will speak in short phrases with a stoic expression because they were trained that way. There is a theory in adult learning, "What you learned first, you learned best." If you first learned to be brief and stoic with a "just the facts" demeanor, you learned that very well. However, in a promotional test, you will receive lower scores when non-military assessors are scoring. Unlearning what you learned first is very possible, but it will take more effort than learning what was learned first.

Understanding your audience is the reason to adapt your style to better connect with them. How do you know that you are connecting with the audience? You will feel their warm response that comes to you by their non-verbal language. If you do not feel it, you may not be connecting with them.

Stay focused on the main themes or core parts of your message and use themes that you crafted while preparing. Follow the organization and sequence that you envisioned. Stop yourself from going off message and going down "bird walks" that are tangents from the core message. These tangents are tempting to go down but may lead to the impression that your thought process is impulsive and disorganized.

13. <u>This is not the time to be a minimalist or arrogant.</u> Some of this was covered in the previous section about some military veterans. We have seen great candidates who used 100 words to tell a 1,000 word story and this left the assessors with very little to score. On the other hand, nearly everyone is turned off by the talker who is selfish, boastful and arrogant. There is a middle ground where you will find effectiveness. Think about this continuum of characteristics that candidates fall in and their style of oral communication. It also marked as a *Key Theme* to remember and use.

- Minimalist
- Shy
- **Humble and Confident**
- **Talks Positively About Others**
- **Gives Credit and Accepts Blame**

- Self-centered and Boastful
- Arrogant

The lower scoring communicators are the two on each end of the spectrum: minimalist, shy, self-centered, boastful and arrogant. The higher scoring speakers are Humble and Confident, Talks About Others and Gives Credit and Accepts Blame. Let's drill down on these.

Humble and Confident is the candidate who plainly yet proudly talks about the accomplishments made. Rather than using the word, "I," their narrative is dominated by the world "we." Confidence is being self-assured, their actions are rooted in the commitment to values and principles and the listener can draw the line or the path from actions to values.

Talks Positively About Others is the story of what the partnership or the team accomplished. The narrative includes the feelings of why the event was important, what the team members did and how it made the speaker feel. Telling a story about someone else is really a story about the storyteller without having to plainly say so.

Leaders Give Credit to others for accomplishments done by the team because they are self-confident and accept their place in the universe. Based on a foundation of strength, these candidates are unwavering in the notion that "No one is smarter than all of us working together." They do not need the applause that follows accomplishments because attaining the goal and watching the team become stronger is what drives them.

Leaders Accept Blame for the mistakes or the failure to reach a goal because they know that only they are ultimately responsible. They may know that a team member did not do their job but they do publicly blame that person. A leader is responsible for the outcome. I watched a Sheriff take responsibility when a member of his SWAT team killed an innocent person during the service of a high-risk search warrant that was done at the wrong address. The whole controversy went away when the highest-ranking member of the agency took full responsibility.

IN-BASKET EXERCISE

The in-basket exercise remains one of the most common exercises at an assessment center because it can effectively bring out the core skills of assessing information, using judgment to determine priorities, making decisions, delegating work and presenting all of this with an oral presentation. The in-basket is widely used for all positions.

The in-basket for a supervisor's test is typically 12 to 18 individual items and covers a broad set of topics that are centered around getting the work done today, addressing immediate problems & questions, handling team issues, responding to individual employees, solving minor performance issues and doing the assigned work from the leadership team.

The in-basket for the manager is more complex with 9 to 15 individual items with the issues centering on budget, personnel, policy, labor, and issues from the community, elected officials and department heads.

The in-basket is a job simulation that is often framed in the context of being away from work for a few days and coming back to find:

a) Emails. A sampling of examples could be emails from subordinates, other supervisors, the leadership team, citizens with concerns or complaints, agency partners like the prosecuting attorney, the jail, and the vehicle repair shop,

b) Voice mails. Sometimes it will be an actual audio recording or it can be the text of a voice mail. The examples of this are the same ones used for emails,

c) Agency documents including memorandums, case reports and the agency's written forms of notice of sickness, request for leave (vacation, comp time, family medical leave, etc.), request for training and request for equipment repair or replacement,

d) Notes on your desk. Examples might include an employee who is late or sick, something is not working, the boss is looking for you, or a subordinate came by to see you and wants to talk about something,

e) An article from newspapers or magazines to read and prepare for an upcoming meeting,

f) A video clip taken from the media, a cell phone or a body worn camera, or

g) Observations of something that you saw or heard today on the way to your desk. This could include the appearance or demeanor of an employee, something that you overhead, or a piece of equipment that is not working.

PREPARATION TIME FOR STUDY, DECIDE & ACTION

The in-basket is typically a two-part event. The first part is the prep time for studying, determining the priority and making decisions on what to do, who will do it and how it will get done. Sometimes there is a component of writing emails included. The second part of the job simulation is to prepare and verbally present your assessments, decisions, actions and the reasons behind them to the assessors in a continuous verbal narrative – more about that later.

The prep time for an in-basket ranges from 60 to 90 minutes and you will be working alone with only access to the materials provided. This is often realistic, as supervisors and managers often have to make initial judgments on incomplete information, under a time deadline and under stress.

Some test providers put the in-basket prep time as the first activity for the assessment centers. Others have used the time between the other exercises for the prep time. The issues and topics in the in-basket may or may not be in other exercises. So, do not be surprised if the topic in the in-basket is seen again in another exercise. This happens when your employer chooses to have exercises linked together by a common set of facts and these facts are introduced to you at the in-basket exercise.

Let's look at an example of a set of facts in the In-Basket materials that is used in another exercise. At the In-Basket exercise, you receive an email that is forwarded to you from the Commander about a complaint from a citizen of an officer that you supervise. You assess the complaint and make the decision to gather more information by talking to the citizen. The In-Basket exercise is followed by an exercise where you actually meet with the complaining citizen. Then, there is another exercise where you will meet with and counsel the involved employee, and the last exercise where you will write a memorandum that documents the information and actions done in the prior exercises.

The weakness of linking exercises together, like in this example, is also a minefield for the candidate: If a catastrophic error is made in the beginning, like failing to understand all of the facts or placing the wrong weight on the wrong information, the ramifications of that error will likely impact the candidate's performance in the remaining exercises.

> **Key Theme:** Reading comprehension is very important in every exercise. Stay focused, control your nervousness, and be calm and open-minded to the information. Do the assessment of every item in the In-Basket very carefully by reading the material multiple times. Scan all the items first, then read each one carefully and act, and finally, read again and review your work.

Before we talk about the narrative or performance part of the exercise and where the scoring will occur, let's cover in more detail about how to appropriately assess, decide and act because if you do this badly, the best presentation will not save you.

Let's start the study and decide process by talking about how to prioritize and then we will cover assessing, planning, executing and monitoring. One part of the assessor's scoring is determining if you put the items in the right tier of importance. There are typically three tiers of importance: top, middle and bottom. Your goal is to put the items in the right tier, not necessarily in the right sequential order – which is a higher standard and subject to more challenges.

Prioritization is a skill to learn not just for the promotional test but also for the every day work of being the supervisor. The suggestions that follow are intended to also be applied in your job. There is a notable caveat: your agency's subject matter expert determines the priorities. Those priorities may differ with the guidelines presented here because your agency's interpretation and application of the concepts of *Importance* and *Urgency* may be different. What can you do? Learn from the leadership team about their values relating to Importance and Urgency. Then align your thinking accordingly.

Prioritizing begins by scanning and inventorying all the items in the in-basket because you need to know the entire landscape before focusing on a specific item. Spend no more than 60 seconds on each item and put the items into the following scheme that is about ***Importance*** and ***Urgency***. Then be ready to put the items into three initial piles: top tier, middle tier and bottom tier.

HIGH IMPORTANC	**Priority 2: Do Next** Essential communication, staffing, goals & objectives	**Priority 1: Do Now** Health & safety issues of any person
LOW IMPORTANCE	**Priority 4: Later** Review, involvement, input, ideas	**Priority 3: Do Today But Last** Minor employee performance issues, meet deadlines
	LOW URGENCY	HIGH URGENCY

Urgency is more valuable than Importance for the initial sorting.

- Step 1: Put the items that must be done today in the top tier, items that can be done tomorrow in the middle tier and the rest of the items in the bottom tier. The line between the tiers is soft, meaning, you can do things today that are very important and on the list for tomorrow.

- Step 2: order the items within each tier using the criteria of Importance with the most important items before the lesser ones.

Why is this two-step method used? <u>Because being effective is more important than being efficient.</u> The application of this concept separates the candidates who are thinking like a supervisor versus ones who are still master level officers or deputies. Line employees have often mastered how to be efficient in their use of time so they have time to do more work. The average, but lower scoring candidate, will move less urgent items that take less time or effort to the top tier just to get them out of the way. When you are thinking like a supervisor, you keep the priorities straight: urgent issues get the most attention first because supervision and management is more about being effective at accomplishing the mission rather than being efficient with time.

What is effective is to take different items with different urgencies or importance but **involve the same employee** and combine them together into one task. Why? Because the most effective supervisor will look at all the issues knowing that the issues are often related in their cause and then have one meeting with the employee to address all the issues, learn what the root cause is, and develop a comprehensive plan for improvement of the employee's performance. Here is an example:

- The records staff reports that Officer Franklin's reports are often late and are missing critical information.

- The Prosecutor's Office reports that Officer Franklin has not been responsive to their request for follow-up work.

- The range master reports that Officer Franklin has missed two dates for range qualification.

- Officer Franklin has made a short notice request for leave to take their spouse on a trip.

- The evidence staff reports that Officer Franklin is not using established protocol for the processing and handling of evidence.

- Officer Franklin reported being stuck by a needle while searching a prisoner but cleaned it with an alcohol swap from a first aid kit.

You can see that there is a range of priorities in these items. Officer Franklin was stuck by a needle and the wound was treated, this is health and safety issue of blood borne pathogen and that is a top priority. Use this one meeting to address all of the other topics involving Officer Franklin.

This initial sorting of all the items in the In-Basket will work for about 80% of the items. The other 20% will be moved to another priority when you do a second and more thorough assessment. Do not fall into the trap of only scanning the items once and not doing a through and careful read, or using only the subject line in an email to make a preliminary judgment or allowing the "no big deal" tone of a message to sway you.

Rather, be ready to be flexible, adapt and be able to change your mind. Marginal candidates will not see the bigger picture and will get caught up in digging into every item, one after the other until time runs out; leaving items untouched.

Here are some examples of items and suggested priorities that use the scheme above with some pitfalls to avoid and strategies for success:

- An email from the Undersheriff with instructions to read the attached memo from the County Prosecutor and be ready to discuss the implications at the staff meeting next week. This is a bottom tier item because there is no urgency. The mistake by marginal candidates is to put too much weight on the information that it came from the Undersheriff and therefore put it in a higher priority.

- A text from the Principal of the high school, "Hearing a rumor that a student wants to shoot up the school. Can you call me?" This is a top tier item because it is a health and safety issue and you need to immediately gather more information.

- A complaint from a citizen about fast traffic near the elementary school. This is important according to the agency's mission but action on this is not required immediately. Therefore, it is a middle tier or a take action tomorrow item.

- Deputy Olds just called in sick for the next shift that starts in 6 hours and staffing levels are at the minimum. This is a top tier item because of urgency.

- Your boss wants an update report on the effort to reduce crime and calls for service from an area that has many bars and taverns for a staff meeting next week. This is a third tier item because there are more important priorities to do today.

- The manager of the vehicle shop left a "no big deal" voice mail that a bag of needles and drugs were found under the passenger seat during a routine service. This is a top priority item. Do not be lulled by someone else's perception of the priority in making your decision.

With the prioritization done, start working on the highest priority items and use these components of assessment, planning, execution and monitoring to plan your presentation to the assessors. Move through all the items in this manner and pay attention to how much time you have.

Assessment or appraisal of the in-basket items is gathering all the relevant information about each item and making initial decisions. Consider these questions in doing the assessment:

a. Now that the priorities are done, decide if the item is one that **you** have to do or is one that you can delegate. Is the problem or issue one that you have control, influence or jurisdiction over it? If not, then who does? Then your role is to be the bridge to convey the right information, to the right person, in a timely way and tell the involved people what you have done. The rest of this section is about items that you cannot delegate, that **you** have to do. Also, see the next section on Execution about how to delegate a task.

b. Do I have all the resources to move forward? If not, what and who is needed?

c. If the topic involves equipment, is it available and ready for use? If not, take measures to do this.

d. If the involved employees work for another supervisor, you will need to loop them into the process.

e. What employees are needed to accomplish the work and what is needed to make them available?

f. Are the employees who will do the work properly trained, equipped and supervised? If not, what is needed?

g. What preliminary standing orders or directions are needed?

h. Does my boss need to know now or later?

i. If this is a budget decision, are funds available, does this comply with the priorities of the agency, and what approvals are needed? Anyone can say yes to a budget request, the competent supervisor will have the courage to say no when needed. If you going to deny a request, can you give the requesting employee another option?

You will never have enough information to make the perfect decision. Time constraints will require that the best decision is made using the best information available and the information is usually incomplete. Be open to the solution that the assessment showed that no action or decision is required, however, tell the sender that you got their information and what you did and why. A quick way to losing your credibility is not communicating.

Planning. This is under-rated in policing but is very important because like carpenter's say, "Measure twice, cut once." Thinking through the steps and the process saves time and effort, creates efficiency, avoids minefields, and ensures that safety precautions are adequately done.

The best planning process is an inclusive process of listening, earning support and creating a collaborative dynamic with the people who are affected and the employees who are going to do the work. How can you do an inclusive process during an In-Basket exercise where you working alone? The answer is this key theme:

> **Key Theme:** Remember all the exercises are about both DOING and WHAT YOU WOULD DO. "Doing" is the showing or demonstrating the behavior. "What you would do" is telling and explaining to the assessors your actions, decisions and the reasons or principles behind them. You need to be a master at both of these.

Every decision is driven by **time, budget or quality** and these influence all decisions. This includes all the items in the In-Basket. Knowing what is the driving influence will clarify your thinking on how to proceed. Here are some examples:

- When there is an emergency, time is the driver of the decision – get the resources there immediately; quality and budget are secondary.

- When the agency wants to buy a specific piece of important equipment or do an important investigation that is a quality decision; budget and timing are important but often secondary.

- Many decisions are budget driven; when the equipment arrives and if it has all the features desired are secondary.

Knowing that every decision is driven by either time, quality or budget will separate you from the candidates who do not know and telling the assessors what is driving this decision will add to your score. Particularly at the management level, discerning what the driver is becomes more important.

How do you apply a planning strategy to the In-Basket

Exercise? First, use the strategy that is common for any complex process: "Begin with the end in-mind" or what a successful outcome would look like. Without knowing this, it is like starting a trip without a destination. How will you know that you got there? For without a clear objective, any solution will do and that leads to mediocrity and your agency's mission will likely not be achieved.

When the end-objective is known, start working backwards from the end and identify each step that is needed until you get to the starting point. Now, both the steps and the sequence of doing the work are determined. Then work on determining (1) the skills and training needed, (2) which employees are needed, and (3) the resources like equipment, funding, and materials needed.

Execution is the task of dealing with each item. Walk the path of the plan by following the sequence. One point that bears repeating: keep the boss informed on issues that are high liability, involve relationships with elected officials and managers from other departments, and events that may attract media attention. This is important in every exercise and is widely applicable.

Key Theme: The Doctrine of No Surprises is the principle to avoid surprising your subordinates and your boss because it will cause preventable setbacks. Being surprised creates an emotional impact that stops the listening process. When the listening process stops, understanding and agreement will stop with it. Whenever possible, always share what you know as soon as you know it. This keeps the team together.

Perhaps surprisingly, with a good plan the execution is often smooth, seamless and is the easiest part. However, nearly every plan needs to be adapted to new information, new conditions, a new development or a new instruction from the leadership team. So, keep in the back of your mind a phrase from the military, "The first casualty of battle is the original plan."

Deviating from a plan needs to happen to keep the priorities straight which are: health and safety of employees, health and safety of victims, witnesses, complainants and other citizens, and health and safety of suspects. Rigid, black and white thinkers will not adjust or flex and therefore their scores will be lower.

We have said this earlier but bears repeating: execution is about knowing what you need to do as the supervisor or manager and what can be delegated and then acting on it. Supervisors get the work done through other people. Well-intentioned but ineffective supervisors are soloists who insist on doing everything themselves. More about this common mistake in a later chapter.

Delegation is an essential tool of leadership because there is too much to do and not enough time to do it all. Delegation is a strategy to develop employees. If you do not delegate, you will work yourself to death, which your employees will love because there is less work for them, but you will still be dead. You may delegate a task but you never delegate the ultimate responsibility if things go badly. You are the supervisor and the ultimate responsibility and accountability will stop with you.

How do you delegate in the In-Basket? Use these steps in delegation and explain to the assessors that you:

- Made an assignment with a clear list of activities and tasks to be accomplished,
- Gave the employee the authority that is specific to the assignment,

- Ensured they accepted the job and have a full understanding of the expectations, and

- Hold the employee accountable for their role with appreciation and recognition or coaching and in a timely way with a date to check back and verify.

Monitoring is the last task to do for each item in the in-basket. This is the category that is <u>most</u> often overlooked. Why? Sometimes there is so much work coming in that the focus is getting the work out. Sometimes it is "assuming" that the message was received and the instruction was followed. Remember the lesson of making bad assumptions is in the parts of the word ASSUME, "ass-of-you-and-me." Also, monitoring is part of a supervisor's normal thinking. Candidates skip over this because they are not fully thinking like a supervisor.

What does great monitoring look like?

a. <u>Choose the right communication method</u> for conveying opinions, emotion and arguments deliberately and intentionally. The most effective communication strategy is face-to-face, followed by voice to voice (telephone) and the least effective is the written word and especially email. The more important the message about feelings and gaining understanding, the better the communication strategy is needed. A very common mistake is to use the wrong strategy like using email to criticize an employee's performance. Email is great for sending data, objective information, instructions and finalized decisions.

b. <u>Trust but verify</u>. This is especially true for tasks that are delegated. Make yourself a reminder on a calendar to check back with the person to get an update. Ask: what happened, what were the problems, can I help, and for your employees – what lessons did you learn? Use this as an opportunity to express your thanks and appreciation for what they did. Feedback is the breakfast of champions and being appreciated is contagious among the employees.

c. Supervision by walking around. Get out of your office and your car to watch the employees in action. This sends the message that you care about what they do. Simply showing up is the single most effective act of supervision. Go to your partners and the administrative assistants in your agency and other departments who are doing their part of the project and proactively ask, "What can I do to help?" Use this opportunity to listen for improvements and also to express your sincere gratitude for what they do.

d. Inspect. "You get what you inspect – not what you expect." Setting your expectations and talking about these is important but inspection is the powerful tool to put these into action. Inspection is more than just looking, it is also about teaching. If you want clean patrol cars, then inspect them and teach what is expected and how to do it. If you want better case reports, then inspect them and teach how to do better. If you want better relationships with the community, then go and inspect these and reinforce what went well and what could be improved. Inspections are more acceptable to the employees when these are a normal part of doing business and are not surprises. The mistake is to only talk about it and do it rarely.

e. Deal With Performance Issues Now. This is captured well in this phrase, "You deserve the performance that you tolerate." If you do not confront the problem performance, then you are giving your silent consent that it is acceptable and that will create a bigger problem for you. More about this topic in the Employee Counseling & Coaching exercise.

f. Reply Immediately. Send email and text replies that you got the message from a sender. When you do this, the sender will love it and it models the behavior that you want to see in others. Otherwise, your silence could be construed as not caring, ignoring or just being rude.

How do you show this in a job simulation? You tell the assessors **what you would do**.

PRESENTATION TIME

The second part of the In-Basket Exercise may begin with an additional prep time that allows you to put the final touches on your presentation to the assessors. This often happens when the test schedule has a clear separation between the preparation time for study, decide and action and the presentation time.

The oral portion of the exercise may last about 20 to 30 minutes with additional minutes for several interview style questions. You are expected to describe the In-Basket item, what the factors that went into your judgment and decision-making, and describe your actions and orders. You will need to make a full presentation by telling the assessors the results of work done during the preparation period and using the categories covered there. When you do the preparation well, the narrative is explaining that work.

The assessors will not typically interrupt your narrative. Top candidates are comfortable making a narrative to the assessors while receiving little or no feedback or direction for 20 or so minutes. Use the same organization or format to explain each item. You can use the format presented in the preceding section or create your own. When the assessors know what your organization is, it is easier for them to score. Easier to score often translates into higher scores.

To start your time with the assessors, use the tips provided in the **Structured Interview** section. Some highlights: introduce yourself to the assessors, make eye contact and do a sincere handshake, organize your work and start with a confident beginning. Then:

- Describe what the item is, such as an email or voice mail and what the subject is because the assessors need to know this first so they can reference the specific expectations that the agency provided for that item. Many test providers put a page number on the item, which the assessors have in their instructions.

- Briefly explain why this item has its priority ranking. For example, top tier items are urgent life and safety issues. Simply tell the assessors, "This is an urgent safety issue."

- Explain your decisions and actions including what is delegated,

- Answer the "Why" question: briefly explain the reasons including the principles and values behind your decisions and actions.

Use the oral presentation tactics and strategies described throughout this book. Marginal candidates will be uncertain and their presentation will be rambling or be so brief that the assessors will have little evidence to work with.

Key Theme: Be prepared to take the lead in fully describing what you would do and why, and make the narrative interesting. Practice doing a narrative for 20 minutes with a video camera recording you.

A richer In-Basket is a combination of oral and written work. The written work may be to construct a number of emails for items that are identified in the exercise. The assessors will review your written work after the oral portion of the exercise. We will talk more about writing exercises later.

The KEYS TO SUCCESS are:

1. Explain every action & decision as the assessors cannot assume, interpret or predict the reasons you chose.
2. Deal with every item, review and sort them by priority before taking action.
3. Make firm commitments to a course of action knowing that some may be unpopular.
4. Deal with personnel matters decisively yet appropriately. Employees are the agency's most important assets. Separate the person from the issue and be "soft" on the person and "hard" on the issue, if it is warranted.

5. Delegate to the right people by giving them clear expectations, the authority to act and with a time to report back. Doing everything yourself is often not appropriate and the opposite is also true, delegating everything is not taking responsibility for the important or sensitive topics that supervisors and managers must deal with.

6. Some items may need follow-up and cannot be finished with one action.

ORAL PRESENTATION

An oral presentation exercise can come in the form of a shift briefing, an expectations meeting, a leadership team meeting, meeting with a couple of managers, a meeting with a citizen's group, or a meeting with a committee. There can be role players or the assessors can be the audience. When the assessors are the audience, they typically have scripted questions to give you. A reminder from the Chapter 5 on Assessors and Role Players, role players are creating lines from their character. The topics in this group of exercises can range from the very general to an agenda of specific points. After the prep time, the presentation time ranges from 20 to 30 minutes with additional time to answer several interview-style questions.

These exercises are often a true job simulation where you are scored on what you DO rather than explaining what you would do. Scoring often begins when you enter the room and that means **you need to be** the supervisor or the commander. Start your preparation by learning what that mindset is and to develop it. As your preparation for the test continues, this mindset becomes natural and on test day, you are thinking as the supervisor.

Like all materials in the prep area, you can mark up the instructions, create notes, and bring them with you into the exercise room. The typical format is the candidate will take the lead when they enter the exercise room by delivering their narrative and then fielding questions or comments from role players or the assessors who are the audience.

Examples of topics for an oral presentation are:

"Given the attached legal update on search and seizure, make a 15-minute instructional presentation and answer questions."

"Given this article (or this YouTube video) on the use of force, make a presentation and answer questions and concerns at a neighborhood meeting."

"Attached are a set of calls for service and complaints from a neighborhood. Review these, make a preliminary plan to address the causes of the problem and present these to the assessors who are playing the role of managers that you report to."

"Attached is a use of force report. Present your findings and recommendations to the assessors."

For command level positions here are two examples:

"The agency has called a community meeting to address the recent uptick in activities relating to the homeless. Attached is the data from the last three months. Be prepared to present the department's efforts and respond to questions and concerns from the audience."

"The budget sub-committee for public safety is meeting to hear more about the department's request for additional staffing, training and new vehicles. Attached is the Chief's budget memo. Be prepared to present a summary of the memo and to answer the committee's questions and concerns."

Let's talk about several of the exercises in this group and

give you more details on each one.

THE SHIFT BRIEFING

The Shift Briefing is about managing a team or a small group. Team health, dealing with conflict and moving groups into high performing teams is one of the core responsibilities of the supervisor. You will need to read, study and learn about how to do this in preparation for the job. Look up and read about these topics: high performing teams and the theory of forming, storming, norming and performing.

For this exercise, you are tasked to provide a briefing to your subordinates. Usually there are 2 to 4 role players who are line officers or deputies. You may have received some background information on each one. They are wearing nametags so you do not have to memorize their names from the preparation material. You are given several topics to present to the shift, typically issues that the leadership are concerned about, and changes to policy and procedure. Sometimes you are instructed to initiate several of your own topics to present.

Each role player will have a character, a set of lines and questions that each candidate will receive and they will have non-verbal communication to give. You will be challenged in responding to them and addressing their questions and behavior.

The assessors are in the room but are not participating and the exercise begins when you enter the room.

The KEYS TO SUCCESS are:
1. Be the Supervisor in posture, voice, confidence and authority.

2. Represent yourself and the agency well.

3. Though you may be tempted to be negative, keep in mind that you have control of what you do and your professionalism.

4. Be friendly and kind but also firm and fair.

5. Be the model of what a great supervisor would do.

THE EXPECTATIONS MEETING

You are tasked to communicate your expectations as a supervisor or a manager and the audience can either be role players or the assessors. If there are only the assessors, they will be focused on taking notes and will not actively engage with you. Sometimes, you will be provided with some expectations or you are told to provide all of the expectations. You may be questioned or challenged on the need for the expectations or to provide additional clarity about how to achieve them.

The KEYS TO SUCCESS are:

1. How you deliver the expectations is as important as the message. Be optimistic, professional, interesting, committed and confident.

2. The expectations should be realistic and genuine. Use a combination of current professional themes like duty, honor, service and integrity and your agency's mission and values.

3. Communicate to your employees what is important to you from the perspective of the supervisor. To start your journey of discovering this, here are some ideas for expectations:

- Do your job
- Give me your best
- Have a plan
- Continue to learn
- Check the small things
- Follow the process and let the outcome happen
- Challenge yourself and others
- Make a positive difference
- Respect yourself, others and the profession
- Take responsibility for your actions
- Don't do stupid stuff

THE MANAGER'S MEETING

You are given a problem to address and have only the time in the prep area to plan a presentation about what you would do. Therefore, the assessors are not expecting a lot of detail or depth. Rather, they are looking for your knowledge and wisdom in seeing the whole situation, of illustrating that you are not only a leader but also a member of a larger team.

Examples of the kinds of problems are:

- A neighborhood is experiencing a spike in property crime,
- Two officers on your team are using more Use of Force than any one else on the department,
- Team morale is very low and employees are frustrated over a number of issues,

- Businesses on the same block are complaining about the homeless with trash, drugs, arguments and panhandling.

Most often, the assessors are the audience of managers and they will have scripted questions to ask during your presentation.

The KEYS TO SUCCESS are:

1. Own the problem by making it yours and committing all of your skills and talents to a successful outcome. Demonstrating ownership leads to communicating optimism and resolve.

2. Use the expertise, tools and resources at your disposal but also reach out wider and use non-police partnerships like, fire, code enforcement, planning, public works, public health, mental health, etc.

3. The assessor's questions will often focus on why you chose that solution option, what are the budget implications, what is the timing of the effort, and specifically what will success look like. When you proactively address these, it is easier for the assessor to score and often translates into higher scores.

THE CITIZEN'S MEETING

You are tasked with going before a small group of people who are meeting about an issue, a problem or topic of concern. You are representing your agency in providing information, making commitments and answering their questions. In the preparation area, you are given the reason for the meeting, data about the problem, and perhaps the reasons why the citizens are attending.

Sometimes, this job simulation is with a set of role players who have a character to follow, questions to ask, responses to make, non-verbal behavior to show, and presenting their own agenda. Again, you will likely be challenged to explain the reasons why the agency does what it does and respond to complaints or accusations.

The KEYS TO SUCCESS are:
1. Use all of the information in the public speaking skills section that follows along with the tips in the Structured Interview section.
2. Make a good first impression by being confident and have an introduction that conveys your personal credibility and interest in the audience.

Public speaking skills are the core of the oral presentation exercise. Therefore, let's cover this topic.

PUBLIC SPEAKING SKILLS: PREPARING THE PRESENTATION & KEYS TO SUCCESS

✓ Know your information and let your confidence grow from the comfort of having a deep well of good information.

✓ Decide what your core message is and know the purpose of your presentation. Is it only to inform? Or, is also to persuade? With employees, is it also important to gain their understanding and compliance? Knowing the purpose will allow you to harness the right tools and the proper strategy and this will grow your confidence.

✓ <u>Understand that there are different learning styles always in-play</u>. Visual and auditory learning styles are the main ones. The lesser one is kinesthetic where people "feel" the message. When you do not know the learning style of your audience, use visual and auditory messages. Do you know the learning style of your boss and your subordinates? When you do, you will be far more effective. For command positions, do you know how your boss processes information? Meaning, are they a numbers person who often uses a spreadsheet or are they a conceptual person who is grounded by values and principles?

When you tailor your presentation to the learning style of the audience, you will be a more effective communicator. How can you apply this to an oral presentation exercise? Use words to paint a picture, use numbers in some examples, be more animated in your delivery, and use a white board or flip chart to make one illustration that is the most important message.

✓ <u>Have Trust In Your Knowledge, Skills and Abilities</u>. We worry when we do not trust. Worrying creates anxiety that blocks your ability to use all of your skills and talents.

✓ <u>The "3 Meetings" Dynamic.</u> For every scheduled meeting, there are really three meetings to be ready for: (1) the meeting before the meeting which is relaxed and informal and this is an opportunity to learn who is in the room and what their agenda is, which provides an opportunity to address it before the, (2) the scheduled meeting which is more formal with people working their agenda and often playing a role, and (3) the meeting after the meeting which is the opportunity to provide clarification, build relationships, and listen.

Why is any of this important? Marginal participants come to only the scheduled meeting. Top tier leaders come early and stay late to be present and engaged at all three meetings. Being present at the meeting is important because you will hear new information and you have the opportunity to share you voice to shape the outcome, or better said, "If you are not at the table, then you are on the menu."

How does any of this apply to a promotional test? Understanding the dynamic of three meetings can make your answers richer and deeper. Also, when the assessors ask, "Is there anything else you will like to add?" Explaining this concept at the right opportunity could be a great answer that illustrates you depth of understanding and wisdom.

✓ <u>Have water on-hand.</u> Keeping your mouth and vocal cords wet will raise your comfort and keep the best qualities of your voice.

Delivering The Presentation And Keys to Success

✓ <u>Introduction.</u> If the group is small, like at an exercise, introduce yourself by name to each person. Make the introduction genuine and sincere by briefly pausing to greet and look at each person with a smile.

- ✓ <u>Bring you passion, emotion and purpose</u> into the presentation. This separates the great candidates from the good ones. Two flaws to avoid are not showing enough passion, emotion or purpose and doing too much of these. Passion, emotion and purpose are like the great BBQ sauce. With the right amount, it will make the whole meal memorable, but too much is overwhelming.

- ✓ <u>Act like an "owner" of your agency</u> and a partner with the leadership team.

- ✓ <u>Share yourself,</u> not just information. Make eye contact with every member of the audience. Do this by scanning back forth and take in the whole room. A smile is the shortest distance between two people.

- ✓ <u>Your body language sends a message</u> that has more impact than your words. Then your voice tone, volume and pacing determines if your message is interesting. The roots of these come from your passion, values, purpose and your self-confidence. These are grown, honed and polished with practice. Again, beware of distracting mannerisms like clicking the pen, slouching in the chair, and saying "Umm." How do break these? By practice and getting feedback.

- ✓ <u>How you start and how you finish</u> is what is remembered after the meeting is over. Never begin with an apology even when you are a last minute substitute. Instead begin with a genuine compliment about the audience. End the meeting with a summary and an expression of gratitude.

- ✓ <u>Never let the audience see you sweat.</u> Public speaking and being in the hot seat is stressful. Wear your game face of being calm and confident. Be prepared with knowing what the difficult questions might be. Have more than enough handouts and business cards ready. If you are using a microphone or a projection system, pilot test all of them before the meeting starts. Acknowledge difficult questions and take difficult people outside of a group and meet them one on one. There is a time to say with courage, kindness, authority and respect:

"I do not know the answer right now, but I will find out and get back to you."

"This sounds like you have important things to share with me. Let's meet later so I can better learn and respond to your concerns."

"I am going to take this under advisement and get back to everyone later."

✓ Use the big three elements in your presentation: **Stories** because we are drawn to good stories by the skill of good story telling, **Humor** and the best kind is always about you and **Enthusiasm** because this is the connector that binds the listener to you.

✓ Do not make stuff up, throw others under the bus, or be the unhappy employee. Never compromise your integrity or make promises that you cannot deliver. Instead, take a lesson from successful businesses, "Under promise and over deliver." Meaning, make a promise that is easy to deliver and then exceed their expectations.

Ways To Finish And Afterwards

Finishing well leaves the audience satisfied and upbeat and at the assessment center is the springboard to a good score. How you do this is best done as a part of your preparation by making some decisions and then practicing your delivery. Some ideas to consider are:

- ✓ Provide a summary of what was learned and what will happen next,
- ✓ Speak to why this meeting or topic was important and weave in the mission and values of the profession and your agency.
- ✓ Express your gratitude for their time, care and involvement.
- ✓ Give your business card with eye contact, a smile and a handshake. This gesture is still effective at the test when you do not have a real card to give.

Every presentation is a learning experience and getting feedback is essential. As Dale Carnegie said, there are always three presentations: the one you practiced, the one you gave and the one you wished you gave. Learn but do not dwell on your performance with in-depth self-critiquing during the promotional test because this may affect how you do on the other parts. Instead, think like the supervisor or manager, breath deeply and move on.

The KEYS TO SUCCESS are:

1. Unless a specific agenda is provided, prioritize the materials provided and cover them in order of importance.

2. Unless otherwise instructed, you may add other items to the presentation that are relevant to the time, the region,

and the audience. However, these should be real and not fictional. "Making stuff up" often results in a lower score.

3. Start with a strong and confident beginning.

4. Your voice volume should reach to the back of the room where the assessors often are.

5. Have a clear and concise theme of what you want the audience to remember.

6. Provide objective supporting evidence for your decisions or actions.

7. Be organized and structured; know the direction of where you are going with the presentation.

8. Watch your time. Use all of it wisely while not being rushed, adequately covering all the points, and answering all the questions. Speaking faster is not always better.

9. Your delivery should be easy to hear and understand

10. Practice with a video camera even though it is hard to do. You will discover mannerisms and delivery issues that can affect the message and are preventable. Are you a pen clicker? A desk drummer? A sloucher? Do you over use, "Ahs, OK's and Umms? Stop using filler phrases such as "like," "You know what I mean" and "I apologize."

11. Be serious and act like the supervisor or manager. Marginal candidates will use trite phrases, "That is above my pay grade."

12. Your voice should not fade out at the end of a sentence.

13. Have a strong finish and stop.

EMPLOYEE PERFORMANCE MEETING

Nearly all assessment centers have this job simulation and most other processes will have this as a topic that you will be asked about. Also, agencies choose this exercise because one of the chronic weaknesses in all organizations is effectively dealing with employee performance issues. Being a supervisor means routinely meeting with employees for purposes like: to resolve a performance issue, teach, give direction, set expectations, provide assistance and show appreciation and support.

As with all of the job simulations and exercises, you are expected to act like you are in the position being tested for and you possess all the duties, responsibilities and authority that accompanies the position. We have said this repeatedly because this message is so important: Top candidates will **be** the supervisor in a heart-felt way: in their words, their posture and presence, their attitude and how they think.

Key Theme: Know your agency's policies and procedures regarding what the position is responsible for and how specific duties are carried out.

In this exercise, you are tasked with meeting a role player who is playing the part of an employee and to address a performance issue that is appropriate for this position. The issue is not a criminal investigation, does not rise to a formal internal or administrative investigation and does not end with a suspension or termination. At its core, the exercise is confronting an issue and providing coaching and counseling.

It is common that you will receive a description of the performance issue and some background information about the employee in the prep area. Also, you will learn if the employee is waiting for you in the exercise room or will be coming in after you.

The exercise room is intended to represent your office or a conference room and typically the assessors will not participate when the role player is present. Be sure you have reviewed the chapter on assessors and role players.

The length of the exercise is shorter than a real-life employee meeting. That means there is very little time to warm up to your A-game or spend a lot of time building rapport, reviewing information, being persuasive or building a relationship of respect and trust. In a real situation about 20% of the time is spent doing these because you need to live the principle that you really care about the employees. However, use the time in the exercise room to touch an all of these. Be direct in your message, but not directive in your style. To be most effective, the top candidate will have a plan to meet the goals of the meeting. In your preparation before the test, you can learn what the plan should include and practice it and that means researching what good coaching and counseling looks like.

Common to most employee performance issues is low morale. Either the core problem is low morale or there are other issues and low morale is the result and most visible symptom of a problem. Morale is more than just the employee's feelings about the job; it is linked to how the employee feels about themselves and their life. Low morale is often about the lack of hope; hope that their frustration will go away, hope for a better assignment, hope that the job will be better, and in general, life will get better.

Hope-starved employees will follow anyone who will feed them including bad leaders and complainers. Your role as the supervisor is to convey optimism; that no matter how bad things will get, they will always get better. The central method to teach this is by your attitude. Said in another way, you must be the model that you want to see in others. Everyone studies their boss. As the supervisor, you are living in a fish bowl where your words, facial expressions, mood and attitude are all carefully examined.

Being a positive influence and being optimistic means that you cannot show that you are having a bad day and you cannot complain. Because if you do, that is sending the message that the behavior is acceptable for them to do too. Making the transition from master officer or deputy to the supervisor also means shedding bad habits.

After the role player leaves the exercise room, there is often additional time to answer clarifying questions, add information and answer several interview-style questions that are often related to the topic with the assessors. Here is an example:

"Tell us about a time when you coached and guided an employee and what did you learn from that experience."

The intention of the additional questions is an opportunity for you to fill-in-the-blanks about what you would do next and gives evidence of your skills and knowledge.

A common variation of the employee performance meeting is an exercise that involves two role players, an employee and a manager where the manager has authored a memo about the employee's performance issue. The candidate meets first with the employee for about half of the exercise's time, then meets with the manager who has questions, provides a briefing, and answers their questions. This variation often focuses on the candidate's ability to demonstrate their courage in dealing with the performance issue with the employee and the courage to give new information and persuade the manager that their initial assessment may not be correct.

The KEYS TO SUCCESS are:

1. As in every exercise, pay close attention to the detailed information provided in the exercise instructions. Do not just skim them. The information needed to find a solution is in the instructions and what is learned from the employee. We have seen candidates who did not read all the pages and missed key information that resulted in lower scores.

2. Manage the available time. The assessors may not give you a warning that time is close to running out. Allocating the appropriate time is a reflection of you knowing the priorities and managing the conversation.

3. Attempt to learn what is the root cause of the employee's behavior and this is done by asking questions and listening carefully. There may or may not be an underlying personal issue; it could be a simple issue of laziness, being burned-out and having poor attention to detail. There may be a deeper personal or work issue that may be revealed if the right question is asked. Ask about this only a couple of times and be open-minded and adaptable if an issue is discovered or not.

4. Research and learn about how to do coaching and counseling of employees. There is the **basic employee-counseling model** that is the subject of many books and articles that are worthy of study. Coaching and counseling is a combination of skill

and style. A skill can be learned; your style is acquired over time with experience and experimenting with tools to learn what works for you.

As part of your preparation, learn from master-level supervisors about their style and take away what works for you. One strategy to consider is to incorporate asking more questions instead of delivering only a narrative. **The power of a well-crafted open-ended question** that compels them to be insightful in their answer is far more effective than you telling them what the right thing is. Questions like:

- What happened?
- Why did you do it that way?
- Tell me how your actions reflected the values and mission of our agency.
- How did that decision turn out for you?
- What did you learn from that experience?
- What would you do differently the next time?
- What is your plan to move forward?

The skill of coaching and counseling contains these main components:

✓ Establish rapport. As we said earlier, even in the job simulation exercise, spend a couple of minutes being interested in the employee as a person, before talking about the issue.

✓ Confront the issue (rather than the employee as a pe· and identify the problem. Be careful with the wor⟨ choose. Avoid using the word "You" because it m conversation and the issue more personal and can be taken as this is about them as a person rather than about what they did. When the conversation is personal rather than professional, the employee will probably become defensive, stop listening, and will resist the coaching.

Rather, talk about the issue and what was done. Say how you perceive it and then ask how they see it. Asking and listening is very important and is the most effective method of getting feedback and understanding. You will also learn what happened and their reasons behind their actions. Be open-minded to hear new information.

Be on guard for the *common mistake* of lower scoring candidates: to decide in the prep area what the problem is and be blind to new information from the role player. Communicate your understanding of what they said by repeating back their core messages.

Gaining their cooperation is done by asking for their acceptance that they understand you, "Do you understand what I am saying?" "Does this make sense to you?" Gaining their cooperation is also signaling that you understand them, "I understand that the reports were late because you used sick leave to take care of your family."

Remember that many times the reason for a performance issue can be a misunderstanding of what or how the task was supposed to be done or the employee lacked the information, training or experience to accomplish it properly. Be ready to come to the realization that part of the problem may rest with you or a member of the leadership team.

As a supervisor, one of your core duties is to care about your people. Everyone and especially your employees are going through something in their lives. The best boss has earned the trust and respect of their employees to the extent that the supervisor knows what they are going through. What kind of supervisor will you be? The average boss knows the names of their employees, the above average boss knows the names of the employee's spouse and children, the great boss knows the employee's hopes and dreams and the name of the employee's pet.

Sometimes you may feel uncertain about what to do. Perhaps the employee's reasons for their actions may sound reasonable. If you are too empathetic, you will feel what the other person does. Be cautious that you may accept their reasons and lose sight of the agency's expectations and values. Sometimes our weaknesses are an over-use of our strengths.

How does this pertain to the promotional process? You may be tempted by the role player to go down the wrong path by not showing the courage to make a hard decision or to not deliver a message that is right but unpopular. We usually know what to do. The main challenge is having the courage and determination to do the difficult thing.

✓ Be Supportive. If the issues are about training or needing assistance, then be the employee's full partner in finding the resources. Sometimes the best support is just being present.

✓ Set Expectations. Counsel and teach on what should be done by setting expectations and the reasons behind them. Weave in the mission and values of your agency and profession in these reasons. Do this with a voice tone and behavior that is calm, respectful and decisive. Being uncertain, vague, and mumbling is what lower scoring candidates do. The opposite is also true: the candidate who sounds like a drill sergeant, who lectures and does not listen, will also receive low scores.

✓ Communicate Consequences. Counsel and teach on the consequences if there is no improvement. Be soft on the person but tough on the performance issues and be direct about what you are going to do. Follow your employer's policies on documenting and keeping a record, providing verbal coaching, and including the event in a performance evaluation.

✓ Wind Down With An Assurance Of A Clear Understanding. Ensure that the employee has a clear understanding of everything that was talked about by asking for what they understand from this conversation with a question like, "Please tell me what your understandings are from our conversation." Doing this "brief-back" method will clear up any areas that were missed or vague.

✓ Afterwards, ensure there is improvement by monitoring or inspecting and communicating your findings to the employee in a follow-up meeting that is scheduled before this initial meeting is over.

✓ Keep your boss informed and make a record of this event. Follow your agency's practices on how a record is made. Maybe it is an electronic entry into a program, note in a file, or included in a performance evaluation.

CITIZEN COMPLAINT MEETING

Of all the job simulations, most candidates handle the Citizen Complaint Meeting really well because they have a lot of practice. This job simulation exercise is about dealing with a citizen who is concerned or complaining about a service that the agency provided. The goal of this exercise is to assess your skills in interacting with the citizen that creates a resolution within the agency's expectations. In the prep area, you will receive information about the complaint and about the employee who was involved. If this information is linked to the In-Basket exercise, you will see the same information from that exercise.

This job simulation requires you to assume the role for the position that you are testing for. You will meet with a citizen who is concerned about a service provided by the agency or a community problem. The citizen may be passive or may be agitated and difficult. How you begin sets the tone of the meeting and is the assessor's first impression of you.

Be friendly and gracious, shake the role player's hand and look them in the eye with a sincere smile. Remember, be the professional who is service oriented and listen carefully for information that is new. Listening is not waiting for them to stop talking. Parrot back to them their key words or phrases. Show them that you are sympathetic by saying how they are feeling, "I can see that you are upset by what happened."

Being the police supervisor is different from being the master level officer or deputy. Typically officers do not often offer an apology because they need to control a situation and keep their options open. Being a supervisor means you see the whole picture and from a higher elevation. An apology is not a sign of weakness or taking blame or responsibility. Rather, it is a genuine way to show you are listening and care about them. For example, "I am sorry that this happened to you."

The citizen is looking for a resolution or a commitment to action. Do not make promises that cannot be kept. Instead, make reasonable commitments that fall within your agency's mission and values. You cannot make a guarantee about the outcome of the complaint, such as, "the employee will be reprimanded" or "I can guarantee your property will be safe." What you can guarantee is the process that you have control over, such as, "I will assign an officer to this problem and will monitor their progress" or "I will meet with the deputy, share your concerns and reinforce what our expectations are."

End the meeting with a summary of what you heard, what you will do next, and when you will report back to the citizen about the outcome. Give them a business card, even if you do not have one at the assessment center, but make the gesture anyway.

Do you want to further separate yourself from the other candidates? Say, "Your problem is now my problem and I am going to work it. Here is my direct phone number, call me anytime." Cautionary note: Do this only if you really are sincere. Otherwise, the assessors will pickup that this is only an act and the scoring will reflect this.

Common to nearly all citizen complaints is the theme or issue that the public does not appreciate or support the agency or the agency does not support or care about the community. The strategy to over-come this issue lies in these phrases:

A problem leads to an opportunity,

Opportunity leads to education,

Education leads to understanding,

Understanding leads to appreciation,

Appreciation leads to support.

For example, when employees complain that the City Council does not understand the needs of the police department, this phrase points to the solution; the agency has not taught them. The responsibility for the solution lies with the leadership team and employees to do the work of good and on-going education.

Key Theme: Be the professional who genuinely cares about people, is positive and solution-oriented. Top candidates will "own" the problem, the solution and the outcome, and communicate these to the citizen.

Your attitude with the citizen complainant is very important. A common mistake is to assume that the citizen and the public do not like or support policing and therefore the candidate is defensive and tries to persuade the complainant that policing is important. Nothing would be farther from the truth. The Gallup Poll has been measuring the public's confidence in institutions since the 1970's and nearly every year police have been in the top three of 20 institutions. Only the military and small business has earned higher confidence ratings. Police agencies have consistently earned higher confidence levels than the President, the Supreme Court, public schools, banks, media, labor, other parts of the criminal justice system, television news, big business and Congress. While television news, media and Congress are often the most critical of policing, the public has far less confidence in them.

Another version of this exercise involves two role players. The first role player is the citizen making the complaint about what an employee did. After that role player leaves, a second role player enters and is the involved employee. The intention is to give you a chance to show your skills and abilities in listening to and defusing a citizen and listening to and counseling an employee.

The KEYS TO SUCCESS are:

1. Be the supervisor and be the agency's best representative.

2. Study the agency's values and expectations of performance when dealing with citizens.

3. Be a good listener and establish a connection and rapport with the citizen.

4. Use effective non-verbal strategies, such as matching their stance, stand when they stand, sit when they sit, remove physical obstacles such as a table, be upright, physically attentive and have an open and approachable posture.

5. Find a solution that works for all.

6. Only make promises that are realistic and then schedule a follow-up contact.

7. End the meeting with a summation of what you will do with a commitment to connect with them with the outcome. Make

the gesture to give them your business card, make eye contact, shake their hand and thank them for their time.

8. Pay close attention to the instructions and manage the available time.

WRITING EXERCISES

Effective writing is one of the core skills of a supervisor and manager and therefore is chosen by agencies as a job simulation about half of the time for supervisor and all of the time for manager. However, non-technical writing continues to be a weakness in public safety. The weaknesses include: poorly organized or sequenced, too wordy or too brief, using the wrong words, and poor grammar. Typically candidates with higher education levels write better because they had more practice and received coaching. However, any candidate can be a better writer with learning and practice.

Here are the ways to be a better writer:
1. Write and read every day.
2. Capitalize only when necessary.
3. Pay attention to spelling, because miss-spelling is the surest way to look un-impressive and double check the spelling of names. Spell check is a tool but it will lead you astray.
4. Always keep your audience in mind.
5. Catch yourself from using filler phrases and buzzwords.
6. Know when commas, colons and semi-colons should be used.
7. Take a writing course or seminar.

8. Use formats to organize your work. Here are two examples:
   a. Format A
   - Facts – a listing of bullet points of the relevant objective information
   - Deductions – analysis of what the facts support and includes opportunities and challenges
   - Recommendations – a solution or options to consider to solve the problem or to make something better
   b. Format B
   - Summary – brief and direct that sums up the main points
   - Facts with Analysis – every objective fact is followed by a subjective analysis that includes the ramifications
   - Concerns – the challenges, obstacles and issues that could affect the outcome
   - Recommendations – a solution or options to consider to solve the problem or to make something better
   - Appendix – usually on a separate page with references to policy, procedure, law, websites that have additional information

9. Know your traps of misused words and phrases. Know the difference in using similar sounding words like to, too, and two; you, your and you're; when is "who" used versus "whom;" when "is" is used versus "are," when "which" is used versus "that."

10. Read your writing out loud because if it does not sound right, it probably isn't.

11. Edit, re-write, walk away and let it simmer, then read and edit again.
12. Ask for feedback from good writers.

There are two categories of topics to master:
1. The content, meaning the words and information that is your message, and
2. The construction of the message, which is sentence construction, building paragraphs and the organization of the document.

Quality writing that shows a depth of analysis and clarity of thought becomes more important as you move to supervisor and is essential for the progression into more complex assignments and from supervisor to manager.

Key Theme: Good writing is considered a reflection of clear, focused and organized thought processes and is a learnable skill. Top candidates will effectively write at the journeyman or college level. Develop your writing by practice, have your work edited and critiqued, and read good writing.

Typically, there are three kinds of writing exercises:
1. A timed writing exercise that is part of or linked to a prior exercise where the candidate writes a memorandum or an email about what happened at the job simulation. The writing usually occurs immediately after the exercise and any notes made can be used during the writing portion.

A variation is the candidate watches a video or hears an audio recording that simulates an actual event and then documents what is seen or heard.

2. A stand-alone writing exercise occurs on test day and is timed. The assignment may be specific to a set of questions, a topic or issue or can be non-specific where the candidate proposes a program or solution to a problem. Often, this exercise involves presenting a short oral synopsis to the assessors who are assessing the written work.

3. A pre-test day writing assignment. Usually for management positions the candidate receives a writing assignment that needs to be researched and completed. Typically, the assignment includes specifications to the number of pages, font, font size, spacing and margins. The assessors get the candidate's work on test day. Often this exercise involves presenting a short oral synopsis to the assessors who are assessing the written work.

The writing on test day is typically done on a laptop computer using MS Word that is pre-formatted with margins, spacing, and fonts. Spelling and grammar checks are enabled because this is realistic to the work environment.

Sometimes the document has categories or questions to be addressed to keep a level playing field between the candidates. Other times and especially for management positions, the document is blank.

After the exercise, the document is typically printed immediately with copies for the candidate and each assessor, who can mark it up for scoring. These copies are generally not saved because the scoresheet has the information to support the score.

The KEYS TO SUCCESS are:

1. Manage your time and budget some of it to edit your work. Top candidates will typically compose for 75% of their time and then revise and edit for the remaining time. Marginal candidates will frantically compose for the whole time and will be asked to stop writing when time has expired.

2. Look for the words that sound alike but are used incorrectly because the word processing software program may not catch all of them. These include mixing genders, words that are spelled correctly but are the wrong word for the sentence, such as there and their, here and hear, residents and residence, effect and affect etc.

3. Develop a logical format that is easy to understand. One idea is captured and developed in one paragraph. Ideas flow in an easy to understand sequence from one paragraph to another.

4. Set the stage for the reader and summarize the main points at the beginning. This is not a novel where the main points are a surprise at the ending.

5. Prioritize recommendations and be specific.

6. Utilize objective data and information to support your recommendations and opinions

7. Minimize the use of contractions, acronyms and abbreviations because the assessors may not know their meaning.

CRITICAL THINKING &
DECISION-MAKING EXERCISES

Every promotional process will have some kind of exercise or topics that are critical thinking and decision-making. The critical thinking and decision-making exercises are also known as tactical exercises. The scenarios are typically moderately complex, and realistic to your agency and for the position being tested. This exercise is designed to assess your understanding of the facts and your ability to prioritize, respond, judge and be decisive. This all happens while the scenario is revealed in parts with new information.

Using judgment and decision making skills in the field is very different from routine in-the-building and day-to-day administrative decisions. These exercises are intended to simulate the environment of making decisions under the pressure and stress of limited time, incomplete information, unfolding events that are changing, the need to adapt, and to delegate tasks and responsibilities.

Typically, the scenarios are **not** Armageddon or the once-in-a-career event and these are <u>not impossible</u> to successfully handle. Instead, the better test provider will have scenarios that are moderately complex, multi-dimensional events and have a variety of factors or dynamics. The assessors will have specific expectations for each part of the exercise that are designed or approved by the subject matter expert of what a higher scoring candidate should be able to do.

For each scenario there is at least one path of success but it is not clearly identified and therefore you will need to apply sound principles and your agency's policies, values and expectations.

PREPARATION TIME

Typically, the preparation time is short, about 5 minutes, since there is very little to prepare for. You will know the day, time and location of the scenario and probably the number of on-duty employees or that the shift or team is fully staffed. Remember, you have access to all the normal resources that goes with the position, unless you are told otherwise. The average scoring candidates will forget about the potential of using neighboring agencies and other resources like state law enforcement agencies, task forces, the fire department, transit, schools and public works. The candidate who has not prepared or has not worked a special assignment like detectives, traffic, or the school resource officer will often forget about these assets.

Use the preparation time to re-focus your mindset and attitude. You are the supervisor or manager and must think like one by looking ahead, weighing what the options and contingencies are.

You can expect that the assessors will deliver the scenario by reading the information and perhaps showing a map, photograph or a video. Most test providers will provide you with a written text of what the assessors are reading because in the real world the information coming to the supervisor is often in writing or can be retrieved for review. However, if the job simulation includes radio traffic, there may not be text of that information because it is not realistic.

Let's look at several common exercises.

A HANDFUL OF INDEPENDENT SCENARIOS

In this common exercise, there are 3 to 5 independent events that are not related to each other with each broken into 3 or 4 parts. Typically, you have 20 to 25 minutes to address a total of 12 to 16 parts. Doing the math, you can plan out the time and can see that you will have about 1 to 2 minutes to explain your decisions and actions for each part. However, the parts are not generally timed and the parts are not equal in their complexity. Meaning, that you may spend more time talking about one part than the others. There is only enough time to be clear, succinct and direct with your judgments, decisions, priorities and the reasons for them.

The scenarios are either "in-the-field" that involves a call for service or an "in-the building" event that involves an employee and requires action by the supervisor. Some clients will choose scenarios from one category but most will use scenarios from both. The assessors will deliver one part at a time. After each part is presented, sometimes the assessors will ask a question like, "Describe the issues, your decisions and actions, and the reasons behind them" or no question will be directly asked. Regardless, if a question is asked or not, plainly tell the assessors:

- What are the priorities,
- What you are going to do and,
- The reasons, principles and values behind decisions and actions.

As we have repeated before, the assessors can only score

you on what you do and say. You need to act and think like a supervisor and provide a full, yet concise narrative.

Here is an example of an *in-the-field scenario* and the content of each part:

1. Tuesday at 2300 hours and you are the on-duty Sergeant. Two deputies respond to a domestic violence call. A deputy calls you on the phone to report the aggressor is an off-duty police officer from a nearby city.

2. The deputies call back to you and say the victim is refusing to cooperate, make a statement or submit to a photograph. The injuries are consistent with a push and a slap.

3. The victim says that she is leaving and will not cooperate with any prosecution or action against the suspect. The suspect is also refusing to cooperate. The deputies are convinced that no criminal action is necessary because nothing is going to happen to this case. They also have a professional relationship with the suspect and know him to be an outstanding officer. They want to treat this like a disturbance.

Here is an example of an *in-the-building* event scenario and the contents of each part:

1. Officer Shields asks if he can speak with you privately. He tells you that he overhead student Officer Ann Covington talking to another officer about sexual harassment by her FTO. Shields asks not to be identified and that you keep the information confidential.

2. Several hours later on the shift you meet with Officer Covington and she denies any information about sexual harassment from her FTO.

3. The guild president comes to you and says that he has received info that Covington's FTO has asked Covington out for a date and Covington is scared, not knowing what to do.

4. Covington's FTO sends you a text that he wants to meet with you.

ONE COMPLEX EVENT

This critical thinking and decision-making event is one complex scenario that may change locations, breaks into pieces with multiple scenes and evolves over time. This event is delivered in about 12 to 18 parts where you describe the issues, the ramifications and your decisions and actions to address each part. This is the type of event that will generally feel like one of those hot Friday nights, under a full moon and is on steroids.

Here is an example:

1. It is Monday at 2000 hours. There is a call of a domestic violence assault where the neighbors hear yelling and glass breaking.

2. Officers arrive and find the victim with potentially life threatening injuries and the suspect has left on foot.

3. Officers find a large cache of illegal drugs and stolen property in the residence. An officer recognizes the stolen property from a report taken by a neighboring jurisdiction.

4. Officers learn the identity of the suspect who has a warrant for misdemeanor assault and a history of resisting arrest. The next-door neighbor comes to the officers with a 6-year-old child who ran to them when the disturbance started.

5. Neighbors report that the suspect fled on foot into a wooded area that is a greenbelt. Local police K-9 dogs are not available because they are helping another jurisdiction.

6. 30 minutes later, a mini-market that is 2 miles away reports a car jacking and the physical description of the suspect matches the suspect in the domestic violence call. The owner of the vehicle received minor injuries. The vehicle is headed westbound on a major arterial road. The owner says that a 2-year-old toddler is in a car seat in the back seat.

7. A patrol officer spots the vehicle and initiates a vehicle pursuit westbound in moderate traffic; it is dark, in a commercial retail area and it's cool with a light rain.

8. After 5 minutes, the suspect vehicle goes too fast into a curve, sideswipes an oncoming car that crashes and goes off the road. People in the oncoming car have minor injuries. The road is blocked.

9. The suspect flees on foot in the retail parking lot. A pursing officer falls into a drainage ditch and sprains their ankle and wrist and looses their handgun in the vegetation.

10. Dispatch tells you that the following calls are holding: (a) a two vehicle non-injury accident with a possible impaired driver; (2) a shop lifter is in custody by store

security, is being verbally abusive and the store manager has called twice, and (3) an elderly person with minor dementia has not returned home and is over due.

11. A records check shows the suspect's mother lives about 2 miles away. The mother has called 911 saying her son just arrived, is saying the cops are after him and he has locked himself in the bathroom.

12. Responding officers to the mother's residence say the suspect is refusing to come out, is telling the officers that he wants to take his own life. The mother says that her son usually carries a firearm for self-protection.

13. TV trucks and a TV helicopter have arrived in the area of the mother's house and want a statement from the person in charge.

14. The mother has become very uncooperative with the officers and has ordered them to leave the residence saying that her son is a good boy and would not hurt anyone. An officer says he has a clear shot at the suspect and asks for permission to take it.

TECHNOLOGY PRESENTED CALLS FOR SERVICE

In this job simulation, a set of calls for service are delivered by presentation technology such as a PowerPoint program where you are given a set of events of ranging complexities to assess, prioritize and make decisions on. These calls are presented through an automated means with different spans of time between them. The calls do not occur on the same shift because this scenario is not about call management; it is about knowing principles, values, resources, policy, and procedure. Instead, the calls happen on different days and times because the resources available are different at different days and times. Most calls are independent of each other by day and time.

However, some can be sequential and happening on the same day. This makes each call or part of a call related to each other. An example of how this may be done at a test is:

1. Tuesday at 2200 hours, a burglary just occurred at 234 Pine Street.
2. 2210 hours, dogs barking at 350 Pine Street
3. 2225 hours, vehicle just stolen at 500 Pine Street

Can you see how these may be related to each other?

The KEYS TO SUCCESS are:

1. Communicate in priority order, the proper tasks <u>and</u> the proper sequence to do them. There are key principles in events like this: health and safety issues come first; contain, isolate and control the suspect; slow down the tempo of the event; and stage aid personnel early.

2. Be decisive when action must be taken and <u>own</u> the problem, the solution and the outcome.

3. Take a moment to be thoughtful and then be confident and decisive. Marginal candidates are tentative and uncertain.

4. Keep your priorities straight by putting the right weight on the right information.

5. Establish an incident command post and assemble a leadership team if appropriate.

6. Think the "Big Picture" about what is happening or could happen and how other areas or people are affected by the event. Consider the ramifications of what has happened and what may happen by looking ahead. Marginal candidates will be narrow focused, have tunnel vision and will think like a line-employee. As an assessor said, "Supervisors look beyond their coffee cup, while marginal candidates will just stare at the coffee."

7. Manage not only the scope of the event but also the intensity and pace of the event. Work at slowing down the speed of the event.

8. Delegate work to others and monitor them. Master-level employees will do everything themselves and will be consumed by details. As said before, supervision is about getting the work done through others.

9. Utilize mutual aid partners, other agencies and private sector resources as appropriate. Many scenarios will exhaust your agency's resources. Marginal candidates will often focus only on the resources that they control and will act like they are alone.

10. Remember to keep the chain of command informed as appropriate.

THE KEY THEMES FOR <u>ALL THE EXERCISES</u> IN REVIEW:

- ✓ Pay close attention to detailed information provided in the exercise instructions. Do not just skim it. Read it over several times, highlight key parts, make notes and create a plan. Remember your notes can go with you into the exercise.

- ✓ Remember the "bigger picture" by flying at a higher altitude and seeing all of the pieces, the possible ramifications, and thinking ahead in terms of time but also consequences and resources. Think through the steps and consider "what if's" in your planning.

- ✓ Decide in advance what message you want the assessors to learn about you and practice it.

- ✓ Be prepared to take the lead in fully describing what you did and why. Be decisive on the important issues of life and safety, the welfare of employees and accomplishing the mission. Your decisions should be presented in priority order and with the reasons behind them. The reasons are normally the priorities, from highest to lowest. Make your narrative on point and clear. Be in command, not acting in command.

- ✓ Watch your time. Use a monitoring strategy that is easy. Use all of the time wisely while not being rushed, adequately covering all the points, answering all the questions, but not repeating yourself or over-talking the topic to the smallest detail. Allocating time properly is a reflection of knowing the priorities and managing the conversation.

✓ Be the professional who genuinely cares about people, is positive and solution-oriented.

✓ Learn to write well and continue to practice and hone your writing skills. Have your writing critiqued and apply the lessons offered.

✓ Be the supervisor who has the authority, duties and responsibilities to handle the event.

Chapter 9

Characteristics of Top Candidates, Common Errors to Avoid, and Perfect Preparation

At the end of a promotional testing process, the candidates are often in three tiers: (1) the top tier candidates who are often separated from each other by only a few points or fractions of points, (2) the candidates who are clearly not ready for promotion and have low scores, and (3) the remainder of the candidates who are in the middle and are between the two other groups. The candidates in the middle tier are qualified, have earned adequate scores but have been out-competed by the top scoring candidates. Most of the time, only the top tier candidates will be promoted.

The bottom tier of candidates were either not prepared for the test or simply do have the skill set and attributes to be a successful supervisor. They think and act like the successful and master officers or deputies that they are. Because they do not think like a supervisor, they may have difficulty in accepting their scores and seeing other candidates advance. The middle tier of candidates often have not prepared appropriately or have made some of the common errors that will be discussed now.

Key Theme: What separates the top candidates from the other qualified candidates is the absence of making any of the common errors. Plus, the top tier candidates show both the passion, purpose, enthusiasm and the full skill set to do the job. The lowest scoring candidates will make errors that are described in this chapter.

COMMON ERRORS AND WHAT THE ASSESSORS ARE LOOKING FOR

It is difficult to adequately describe what the assessors are looking for because of the number of characteristics and traits desired and the right combination or chemistry of putting these all together. After years of experience with hundreds of candidates and assessors and knowing hundreds of agency executives and managers, we can only offer a profile that no one candidate will probably have. What follows can be viewed as common mistakes to avoid, weaknesses to be strengthened and goals to be attained.

These are organized as common errors and typical traits and behaviors of lower scoring candidates and **instead,** what top tier candidates look like. From the perspective of thinking, look at the common error as what a master officer or deputy may do and look at what the top candidates do as thinking like a supervisor.

Also, go back to **Chapter 6** that describes the behavioral dimensions and look again at the words and behaviors that higher scoring candidates have and the words and behaviors of lower scoring candidates.

Taken as a whole, all of this describes candidates who make the fundamental error of interviewing and acting from the perspective of the job they have now **instead** of making the shift of thinking to **Being The Supervisor.**

Common Error: *"The Bully"*

This is the candidate who is officious, arrogant or domineering, is often a poor listener, rigid and fails to adapt to new information during an exercise with a role player. This candidate will lecture, bully, or is closed-off to the role player's information. Their behavior does not create a sustaining solution to an issue and will often result in angering or shutting down a role-player.

For example, during the employee performance meeting, the candidate dressed down the employee. The candidate conducted a military drill instructor form of scolding, pointing their finger at the role player's face, refusing to hear any of the role player's information and engaged in a 10-minute long monologue condemning their behavior and describing the discipline that could happen.

Instead, the top candidates will show the balance between being confidently in charge with a command presence that is compassionate and ethical, while being a servant-leader who genuinely cares about the people they work with. They will demonstrate the difference between "acting in charge" and "being in charge."

They will persuade the difficult person to be cooperative through their effective verbal and non-verbal communication strategies. For example, rather than seating across a table from the citizen or employee, they will sit next to them. They will engage with the role player by offering conveying care and support and offering solutions rather than just quoting policy and procedure. They will be in-charge, not through a monologue, but by demonstrating confidence, self-discipline and being calm and reasonable. The top candidate will listen and understand the core message of the role player and will be solution-oriented in a manner that creates cooperation and teamwork.

Common Error: *"The Wimp"*

This candidate is perceived as being indecisive when they act frozen, uncertain, wavering, and always needing direction from their supervisor. This candidate is paralyzed by the idea of taking a risk, cannot take decisive action with incomplete or vague information or cannot make a decision alone. They lack the courage and resolve to make a difficult choice or to overcome obstacles.

For example, during a critical thinking and decision-making exercise, the candidate stopped after receiving the third layer, put their head in their hands and stared at the floor. The assessors waited for the candidate to continue.

Instead, the great candidate has a wealth of experience to draw upon, has the mastery of technical skills, and can effectively assess a range of situations that creates a set of solutions to choose from. They are comfortable making decisions with incomplete information because their experience "has taken them there before." They can choose from the options and their decisions are rooted in the values and principles of the profession and their agency.

They have the courage and the self-confidence to act. They will often be ahead of the assessors in the sense of anticipating what the next layer could be and are proactive in addressing the next problem. They are adaptable and unshakable in their resolve to address an unfolding event and are committed to seeing a successful resolution.

Common Error: *"The Soloist"*

This is the candidate who does everything themselves and will not delegate to others. The candidate is often a master-level line employee who will not trust others to do a task as well as they can. They act with a high level of confidence in getting all of the work done themselves. They may be good lecturers but typically are not good instructors and do not really trust other employees to do the job or reach their expectations.

For example, during an In-Basket Exercise, the candidate does not delegate any of the tasks. They will attend every meeting, write every email, make every phone call and do all the research. They will do every task and assignment without asking for advice from peers or getting more information or notifying their supervisor when doing so would be appropriate.

Instead, the top tier candidate demonstrates that an effective supervisor understands that their job is getting the work done through other people. Delegation is more than just spreading the work around. It is about communicating expectations, teaching processes and skills, demonstrating trust and being present to help the employee overcome obstacles.

They understand that feedback to subordinates is the breakfast of champions. The top candidate is a master at creating and sustaining teamwork. They will collaborate with their peers and partners, keep their supervisor in the loop, and will use the challenges and tasks as opportunities to develop others.

Common Error: *"The Renter"*

This candidate does not take ownership of an issue or a problem. They may have the skills, talents and abilities but they do not have the depth of care, loyalty or commitment to the agency, the community or the profession. This candidate behaves like a visitor in someone else's house: they are friendly, courteous and will follow the rules but they are not going to address problems or care about the future of the house. This candidate is not an owner and will move issues and problems to others and push the hard decisions that are appropriate for them to handle, up the chain of command.

They typically do not genuinely care about a subordinate unless there is a prior relationship. Their ability to create and encourage teamwork is directly tied to their friends. Their depth of care and empathy with a citizen is only skin deep because that is what their boss is expecting. They are good at bringing up problems but will rarely offer a solution. When the "renter" is given a task, they will not take any responsibility for effectively explaining it or persuading others to support it. Instead, they will say, "The boss wants this, therefore we will do this." Renters will "throw others under the bus" and will not follow-up to ensure that a solution is found.

Instead, the top candidate is an "Owner" of their agency and is committed to the profession and the leadership team and they demonstrate this by being aligned with the right and ethical actions of the leadership team and being proactive. They drive their training and career development to match the agency's needs.

This candidate is sincere and genuine in showing care and concern for an employee or citizen and consistently does the right thing for the right reason. They are proactive in identifying and handling small issues without the need for direction. They are not looking for recognition for their efforts. They want to be a part of a successful and striving team.

They are committed and invested in the mission of the agency and being a part of the effort to attain goals. Therefore, their thinking is wider, looking further ahead, and grounded deeper in the agency's values and principles. Candidates who are owners, use words like, "our" versus "mine," "we" instead of "I" and the word, "us." Owners will accept responsibility for the problem, the solution and the outcome as theirs.

Common Error: *"The BMW"*
(for Bitcher Moaner Whiner)

This candidate assigns blame and is the scorekeeper of all the wrongs that has been done, will not forgive and forget, and will complain about other employees or members of the agency's leadership team. They focus on the negative and being critical. They view their world through a lens of injustice and unfairness, of us versus them, of suspicion and skepticism, are not hopeful or optimistic and being victims of someone else's actions.

This candidate often succumbs to the temptation of spreading rumor and speculation and will not buffer from others the accusations they have learned from others. They are not confided in and are typically not trustworthy. These candidates often have poor impulse control and few personal filters; what they think is what they say and will often not have thought through a position or opinion.

For example, during a Citizen Complaint Meeting, they will tell a citizen that the city council does not provide the funding to solve their problem or that the employee was wrong even though they have not talked with the employee. Their response to an interview question will portray the leadership team as "them" who are out of touch with the line employees and are the cause of agency's problems.

Instead, the top-tier candidate will value their relationships with all employees and citizens and will act in a manner that conveys their genuine care for them. They will take responsibility for their agency because they genuinely believe that they are part of a team, a team that shares success and credit and accepts criticism together. They value the trust put in them by others, will convey hope and are optimistic that things will get better.

They are thoughtful and measured in their responses that could be critical. They are loyal followers of the right and ethical actions of the leadership team and will align their leadership efforts with them. They are buffers, not conveyor belts, for other employees and they are respected for being good listeners and will keep private issues confidential. They show their teeth as a leader, both in the smile of gratitude of being an advocate and the bite of accountability.

Common Error: *"The Insider."*

This is the candidate who over-uses words and phrases that is slang or acronyms that are agency-specific and may be foreign to the assessors. This candidate has made the mistake of failing to know and adjust to their audience. If the assessors cannot understand the message, the value will be lost. The merely adequate candidate will talk only about the text of the policy and procedure but miss the bigger picture of the values and reasoning behind it.

For example, during a Shift Briefing exercise, the candidate addresses a number of topics with explanations and uses "insider humor" and slang terms to identify procedure, people and places. All of these are lost on the assessors.

Instead, the top candidate will know and can articulate the broader themes of the root principles behind the agency's policies and procedures and can explain why the agency does what it does. They have the depth of knowledge, have done their personal analysis that results in their acceptance of the principles that drive the agency. They have embraced the mission, vision and values and will weave these into their responses in a genuine manner. This is more than just studying the science of supervision; this is having the heart and the art of being the supervisor.

Common Error: *"Tunnel-Vision."*

This is the candidate who ignores or cannot see the bigger picture and the ramifications of their decisions. This candidate is only concerned with the very immediate needs of the situation and their decisions are typically perceived as being shortsighted and only deal with the signs and symptoms presented in the near-term. They do not look ahead or think about contingency plans. They operate under a misguided set of assumptions that what has worked in the past and in their current position is good enough for the position they are testing for.

For example, during an employee performance meeting, the candidate focused only on the employee's missing deadlines and being late for work. The candidate missed the clues that were underlying personal issues, which the candidate had been counseled before, and an important court date had been missed. The candidate's solutions were narrowly focused on a few issues and they missed the wider issues.

Instead, the top candidate will listen carefully and thoroughly digest the written information and will consider new information. They can articulate the impact of what their decisions will have on others, what is needed in the near term, and what other options will be available. They will accurately identify the most important issues and will identify the root cause of issues.

They will have sound, reasonable and attainable strategies on how to address problems and setbacks. The marginal first line supervisor candidate will think in terms of minutes; the adequate first line supervisor candidate will think in terms of minutes and hours; and the top tier first line supervisor candidate will think in terms of minutes, hours and days. The top tier manager or executive candidates think in terms of weeks, months and years.

Common Error: *"The Pit Bull"*

This candidate is often unable or unwilling to receive, accept or adapt to new information. This candidate will frequently lock onto one piece of information, fail to hear or assess new information and will make decisions from that one perspective. They often put the wrong weight on the wrong information. They will skip over, ignore or fail to see important details. They are typically poor listeners because they are pondering their reaction to the information that they have locked on to.

For example, during an employee meeting exercise, the role player said he had no regrets about his actions. The candidate locked on to this response and failed to hear about the employee's other information of having personal problems at home, being in conflict with other officers and being discouraged about not getting a special assignment.

Instead, the best candidate is patient and calm throughout the meeting and takes notes to remember the important information. This candidate asks open-ended questions and repeats important details back to the employee to demonstrate listening and understanding. They have used tools like a highlighter to remember important information that was in the instructions. They are continually assessing the information. They base their judgments and decisions on all of the information.

Common Error: *"The Conveyor Belt."*

This candidate has lost their focus of providing the highest quality of service. This candidate will focus solely on the <u>process</u> of getting the work done and not consider the <u>outcome</u>. They are more concerned about efficiency rather than effectiveness. They are good at talking about ideas and concepts but cannot execute and deliver. Their narrative will describe in detail the stages of planning and the steps of moving work through the agency. Their measurement of success is the fulfillment of procedure and there is no mention of, or effort made on the topics of quality, meeting a deadline, staying within budget or what the desired outcomes are.

For example, during The Manager Meeting Exercise, the candidate addressed a number of crimes and quality of life issues in a neighborhood. The candidate spoke in detail about the stakeholders, identified the tasks to accomplish, and the methods to communicate. They glossed over or missed completely what success looks like, the budget ramifications of their strategy, the time scheduled to accomplish the benchmarks or how it will be measured.

Instead, the great candidate will honor the process, create teamwork while being solution-focused, and be concerned about the quality of the work performed. They know that quality work comes from dedicated and professional employees who are appreciated and are free of distractions and obstacles. These top candidates do not assume that the work is first-rate; they will inspect, verify, follow-up, check back, see for themselves and will close the information loop by keeping their boss informed.

Common Error: *"The Robot"*

This is the candidate who is perceived as reciting a memorized text, over-uses the current buzzwords, is stiff and wooden, rigid, black or white in their judgment, and their delivery is flat and uninteresting. Or, their narrative will be rapid-fire, disorganized and wandering as they try to repeat the themes that they have studied but probably do not genuinely believe.

This candidate may have studied the science of supervision and management but probably does not have the heart for it and has not started developing their personal <u>art</u> of supervision and management. They view their preparation like an actor who is studying for a performance; they rehearse the superficial but do not attempt to internalize the knowledge and to grow, change and evolve.

This candidate is more of a pretender, rather than a contender; is more of a fraud rather than being genuine. Usually, the stress of the promotional process will crack this candidate's façade in a few minutes.

Instead, the higher scoring candidate will show their passion and enthusiasm for the promotional opportunity, their agency and the work. They are engaging, animated, sincere and genuine and are perceived as speaking from their heart. Their energy and motivation comes from their deeply held beliefs and principles.

Their explanations are easy to understand because they have a deep well of experience and knowledge from which to draw from. Their actions are surgically precise and efficient because there is no wasted effort; simply, they just know. Supervision is both an art and a science. Learn the science and discover the art. The science is information and techniques that can be learned. The art comes from your values, beliefs and judgments and is expressed in your passion. The science is being head smart; the art comes from your heart. The science is saying the right thing; the art is intending and doing the right thing.

Common Error: *"The One Dimension Candidate"*

This is the candidate who has a great amount of experience in only one area and they see every fact pattern, every problem and every option through the lens of their narrow experience. Their answers and judgment are limited as they lack the breadth to adequately see the whole picture or they have blind spots and miss critical opportunities.

For example, a candidate spent years serving in the leadership of the union and they viewed every situation during the In-Basket Exercise as a potential violation of the union contract. Another example, a candidate served for years in a search and rescue assignment and when faced with responding to a potentially complex and unfolding crime scene, the candidate did not have the appropriate breadth of technical knowledge.

Instead, the great candidate will have a broad spectrum of experience and acquired knowledge to draw from in crafting their answers and actions. Their effort to prepare for the promotion began long before the promotional test and they intentionally found opportunities to learn and experience many aspects of the job of supervisor. They are drawn to the opportunity to use their talents and efforts in serving the organization and the employees by being a leader. Everything this candidate has done has prepared them for this opportunity.

Common Error: *"The Failure"*

This candidate either perceives that they did poorly in an earlier exercise or that they are not qualified or able to be a supervisor. Either way, they let that perception color their performance in the other exercises. This candidate is shaken to the core by their perception that they did not measure up to their own expectations and are unable to separate the exercises into truly independent events. They have placed too much weight on their interpretation of negative feedback from an assessor.

They focus on their shortcomings and lack the confidence that they can do well. They become easily discouraged, lose momentum and their discouragement weighs them down. They conclude that they will not finish in the top tier of candidates. This candidate is unable to let go of their judgments and perceptions that they "failed" an exercise.

For example, during the Structured Interview exercise, the candidate perceived that they lost focus while answering a question and rambled. They decided that the assessors were critical of their responses because the assessors never made eye contact with them and one of the assessors shook their head indicating that their answer was weak. The candidate knew that that they did not manage their time well because the assessors gave a warning that only three minutes remained and there were three more questions to answer.

After the exercise, the candidate was discouraged and upset. They spent their time before the next exercise analyzing their performance, picking it apart and seeing all of their shortcomings. The list of what they should have done was far longer than the list of the good responses. During the prep for the next exercise, the candidate could not shake the feeling that they had failed the whole promotional process. When the candidate started the next exercise, they were subdued, hesitant and uncertain.

Instead, the top candidate knows that perfection is something to achieve during preparation but will rarely, if ever, be accomplished at the promotional test. They understand that perfection of effort is the goal rather than earning a perfect score. They have the experience of living through a setback by continuing to focus, applying their best effort, and keeping their sight on doing their best at every opportunity.

The top candidate understands that there will be plenty of time later to analyze and be self-critical after the promotional process. This candidate has studied the promotional process and understands that what the assessors may be scoring may have nothing to do with their perceived weakness.

The top tier candidate is prepared to receive little or no feedback and the assessors may be cool, neutral and not engaged with their performance. They also have learned from experience that their perceptions of themselves can be wrong. These candidates are always looking ahead, being prepared for the next opportunity to show their skill set, and they have confidence in their knowledge and preparation.

Common Error: *"The Nervous Nellie"*

This candidate worries so much that it is manifested in being so nervous that it detracts from their performance. Some nervousness is healthy because it focuses energy and sharpens the senses. At nearly every promotional process, we saw a candidate who was hyper-nervous and they frequently earned lower scores. Hyper-nervousness manifests itself in different ways:

- The candidate speaks so fast that they are misunderstood by the assessors and their information is rambling, disorganized and incomplete;

- The candidate freezes, shuts down, panics and cannot verbally respond to the scenario;

- The candidate appears to be dis-engaged and is unable to focus and concentrate on the scenario;

- They are sweating profusely, constantly in motion and cannot sit still.

- The read and scan the Candidate Instructions and other documents so fast that they miss key parts.

- The candidate has non-verbal mannerisms that are distracting like shaking their keys, rocking back and forth, swiveling in their chair, and constantly fumbling with their written instructions and notes.

Instead, the top tier candidate will be focused, engaged and remain calm. They have practiced and prepared through visualizing what they want to do. They are confident and self-assured because they have inventoried their strengths and worked on their weaknesses. They will pace themselves, keep an eye on the clock, and listen for new information. Essentially, they will be totally present with the role players and the assessors. They will act natural, genuine and authentic, prepared and they will remain centered, focused and adaptable as the scenario unfolds.

DO A PERFECT PREPARATION

Forget about being trying to be perfect on test day because there is too much that is beyond your control. Instead, work on a **perfect effort of preparation**. Preparation means different things to different candidates. The top candidates will do a full range of preparation from learning the subject matter, studying leadership, modeling the performance they want to see in others, visualizing what great judgment and human relations looks like, being mentally and physically ready, and learning about the testing process.

Key Theme: The candidate who is the best prepared, in the areas of commitment, attitude, research, practice, knowledge and has a good history of work performance, is often in the top tier. As NFL Quarterback Russell Wilson said about the separation between good and excellence, "Separation is in the preparation."

Your **perfect preparation** should include these:

✓ Understand the fundamental elements of the job by studying the job description.

✓ Commit to understanding all the information provided about the exercise that was in the instructions, not jump to conclusions about what the exercise is about, and not have a preconceived notion of the exercise.

✓ Ask questions that are needed for clarification.

✓ Think and act like a supervisor by being in the mind-set, the role and doing the duties and responsibilities of the position.

✓ Communicate clearly with sufficient explanation and detail their actions and the reasons behind their decisions.

✓ View the exercises as the "real thing" and not hold back on their performance.

✓ Know their professional resume and be able to clearly articulate the most important aspects of their qualifications.

✓ Study the assessment center and promotional testing process.

✓ Understand the direction and priorities of their agency.

✓ Learn from others who have participated in an assessment center or promotional process.

✓ Seek constructive criticism or feedback from others while training for the promotion.

✓ Rehearse role-play scenarios so the assessment center will not be first time that they have done one.

✓ Study the budget and the priorities of the agency and the community. This is particularly important for managerial positions.

✓ Study the agency's high liability policies because these are often included in the promotional process.

✓ Consider the community and local government issues and how these may impact their agency.

✓ Learn and apply basic English composition skills and continue to hone their writing skills to write at the college level.

✓ Learn and apply coaching and counseling skills and learn from other master-level supervisors.

✓ Learn more about how to manage critical events, what are the main principles, and what are the sound tactics.

✓ Summarize important points in their answers or meeting with a role player.

✓ Take advantage of "anything to add" opportunities from the assessors as a method to provide more detail, reinforce main topics, volunteer why they want this position, or add a new personal theme that clearly communicates their desire for the promotion.

✓ Prepare physically and mentally for "race day."

CONTROLLING NERVOUSNESS

Doing all of the above items will help you be less nervous because you will be more comfortable that comes being more confident. But there is more to do to calm your nerves. Take a hint from musicians, singers and actors: they rehearse and practice for hours. They do it privately but they also do it in low-risk public settings. We are not suggesting that you practice your oral resume on the street corner. However, practice means talking and presenting to others who have agreed to help you. Successful candidates often do not grow into this by being alone; it is accomplished by creating a team of supportive people who will give the feedback and critique that is needed.

Practice means more than an hour the day before the test and practice is not just reading and researching. Consider the ratio of 3 hours of practice and rehearsal for every hour of testing. If the assessment center lasts four hours, be ready to practice and rehearse for 12 hours. The work is the practice; when this is done well, the test will seem easy.

Mentally visualize your performance on test day: what you will wear, how you will greet the assessors, how you will sit, how you will keep track of time, how you will handle questions, how you will deal with role players, and how you will close the exercise and say good-bye to the assessors. Feeling some nervousness is a good thing because it is a signal that you are focused and ready to use all of your skills.

Apply a lesson from officer survival training that pertains

to the mindset for the promotional test. In officer survival training, the color white symbolizes an officer's attitude as clueless and oblivious to the surroundings. The opposite is the color black where the officer is in sheer panic. Yellow is the color for the officer who is relaxed yet alert. Orange is the appropriate focus on the threat and the task to do. Finally, red is the condition where you are totally engaged using all the tools and resources to win.

On test day, you want to be in condition orange and red: completely focused and immediately applying all the tools and preparation to each exercise with a sustained and consistent effort. If you are tired at the end of an exercise and exhausted at the end of the promotional test, then you have probably been in condition orange and red.

Stay focused or keep your eyes on the prize. Rumor, gossip and speculation by the other candidates will likely intensify as the test day approaches. Much of this is rooted in fear: fear of the unknown and fear of doing poorly on the test. Candidates who are afraid often seek validation and support from other candidates. Fear is a powerful emotion that can weaken your preparation by draining your energy, becoming distracted and weakening your self-confidence.

The test is a competition between candidates. Stay focused on your preparation, separate yourself from the rumor, gossip and speculation. All of your preparation for weeks and days is like adding ingredients to a crockpot that is on medium heat. You have been adding and digesting. The day before the test, stop the high intensity of studying and let your crockpot go to simmer. Do a moderate amount of exercise to rid your muscles of the growing tension and use the increase blood flow to clear away those tiny mental obstacles. Use the quiet time to reflect, discern, remember, and commit to being the supervisor.

QUESTIONS TO ASK THE TEST PROVIDER

The professional test provider should be able to answer these questions in a timely fashion before the test and every candidate should receive the same information to keep a level playing field for all of the candidates. Asking questions is not a sign of weakness nor will it cast an unkind light on you; it shows that you are serious and thoughtful. Knowing the answers to these questions is a key part of your preparation:

- ✓ How many candidates will be participating?
- ✓ How many exercises or job simulations will there be?
- ✓ When will the test be administered?
- ✓ Where will the test be administered?
- ✓ What is the attire?
- ✓ What can I bring to the test?
- ✓ How long will the test last?
- ✓ Are study materials available?
- ✓ What is being scored? Such as what are the behavioral dimensions, attributes or characteristics that the assessors are scoring?
- ✓ How was the test validated for this agency and this position?
- ✓ What is the range of points that can be earned?
- ✓ Are the behavioral dimensions, attributes or characteristics weighted?

✓ How is scoring done, by exercise or by behavioral dimension?

✓ Is there a minimum passing score?

✓ Where do the assessors come from and how are they trained?

✓ Are there supervisors or managers from my agency in the exercise? If so, what is their role?

✓ What test materials can I see after the test and when can I see them?

There is a lot to prepare for if you are viewing preparation as a sprint within days or weeks before the promotional process. However, if you are working a well-developed plan to be the next supervisor or manager, then this preparation is more like a marathon where you have been training everyday. Now, use all of the information in this chapter and the next to create your plan of preparation to *Be The Supervisor*.

THE KEY THEMES IN REVIEW:

✓ What separates the top candidates from the qualified candidates is the absence of making any of the common errors.

✓ The candidate who is the best prepared, which includes commitment, attitude, research, practice, knowledge and has a history of good work performance, often is in the top tier.

Chapter 10

Planning to Succeed

"Proper planning and preparation prevents a piss poor performance," is a British army adage that is applicable to the promotional processes. One of the goals of this book is to remove some of the mystery of the testing process so the obstacles caused by extreme nervousness and anxiety will be lower, and therefore, your preparation will be more effective. Preparation begins with crafting your personal plan. In the previous chapter, a number of specific tasks and ideas were presented. This chapter will build upon those and serves as a reminder as you close your preparation and take the final steps to test day. The elements of that plan are in **bold.**

Your attitude about the promotional process and being the new supervisor or manager is one of the most important tools that you have. Decide early what your attitude is going to be. Are you going to be intentional, disciplined and focused? Are you leaving it to luck or divine intervention? On test day, a very narrow point spread often separates the candidates who are in the top tier and the deciding factor is often only one thing: **attitude**.

Are you optimistic, proud and humble? Are you service-focused and servant-oriented or are do you come across as entitled? Are you confident and comfortable or shutdown and defeated? Are you positive and enthusiastic or resigned? Are you boastful and arrogant where it is all about the credit that you are due? Attitude cannot be effectively faked. Assessors will sense a contrived performance, so do not try to pretend or act because failure is surely to follow.

Top candidates **commit all of their efforts** to a perfect preparation and on test day they leave it all on the playing field. They may second-guess their performance later but they do not hold back and will fully demonstrate their knowledge, skills and abilities to the assessors. We often saw candidates who entered the promotional process with, in their words, "to see what the process is and just go through it." These candidates are rarely in the top tier because they lack commitment or passion, that fire in the belly that is the source of energy to persevere and overcome setbacks and continue to learn.

Your attitude and the kind of preparation that you do are the key parts of the promotional process that you have total control over. Take a page from Kevin Gilmartin's book on _The Emotional Survival for Law Enforcement_ and **focus on what you can control** and let go of the rest.

Can you control what the exercises will be? Can you control what the role players will do? Can you control what the assessors will ask? Can you control what the scenarios will be?

Can you control what the expectations will be? Of course, the answer is NO; so do not worry about these. What you do control is doing a perfect preparation.

Be intentional about the message you want to leave with the assessors. This is more than a vague sound bite or commonly heard phrase. This is your personal theme that is intended to be the headline of your professional skills and abilities that sets you apart from the other candidates. It should be memorable and captures your core message that you want the assessors to remember about you. Craft this message carefully, make it thoughtful, personal and heart-felt because there are often opportunities at nearly every exercise to deliver it. Those opportunities sound like questions: "Is there anything else you want to add?" "What else should we know about you that has not been already covered?"

Besides your attitude and your preparation, you also **control your performance** in the promotional process and in your daily life and work. Consider these broad areas of your job performance and work at improving them. Yes, these are the same performance dimensions that many agencies use in the work performance evaluation:

Responsible and Ethical Behavior. This is showing the legal, moral and responsible behavior that meets or exceeds current professional standards. This includes topics like being trustworthy, fair, and honest. Are you willing to commit to a course of action that is right, when it is hard to do or unpopular? Do you proactively admit mistakes before being confronted? Do you sit back and allow others to be irresponsible and unethical? The common failings are being two-faced by giving different messages to different audiences and intentionally ignoring or violating a policy or procedure. Do you give your friends preferential treatment? Do you do the right thing for clients, customers and your agency?

Your Employer's Mission and Values. These are demonstrated through your actions of embracing all of the employer's values, believing in the mission of the agency and taking substantial steps toward attaining them. This is about commitment, being invested, showing loyalty, having a positive attitude and being a great representative of the agency in the community. This is about being a co-owner of your agency, rather than a renter. Do you throw other employees under the bus? Do you criticize the agency's leadership in public? Do you spread rumors and stir the pot?

Demonstrates Quality of Work. This is demonstrating the mastery of the technical skills and meeting or exceeding all of the employer's expectations. Are you proficient in a wide variety of skills rather than just a specialist? Do you consistently do more than the minimum? Can you deliver during the stressful times? Are you consistently meeting deadlines? Do you deliver quality on every task, even the unpleasant ones or only the ones that you like or will receive recognition?

Demonstrates Quantity of Work. This is about doing what is assigned and what you self-initiate and these are done within the expectations of the job. Do you volunteer for other assignments and projects? Are you doing the minimum and is an average worker or are you a star?

Demonstrates Leadership. This is demonstrating effective judgment and decisiveness while working with others that creates teamwork while meeting the employer's mission. Teamwork happens not because people just work together but because there is mutual respect, trust and care for each other. This climate of leadership happens by design and is intentional. Here is a set of questions to do your own self-assessment:

- ✓ Do you model the best behavior?
- ✓ Are you service and servant oriented?
- ✓ Are you a good follower in accepting and following orders?
- ✓ Are you a positive influence on others?
- ✓ Are you optimistic?
- ✓ Do you give credit to others and take responsibility for mistakes?
- ✓ Do you show appreciation for what others do? Being appreciated is contagious and is a powerful way to shape another's attitude.
- ✓ Do you really, really care about the people you supervise? Your subordinates do not care what you know or about your experience, they only want to know if you care about them. Do you authentically embrace people where they are in their life? Leaders take care of their people who will take care of delivering the mission.
- ✓ Do you help others and help create teamwork or are you a lone wolf who would rather do it all yourself?
- ✓ Are you looking ahead, removing obstacles, and encouraging others?
- ✓ Do you have the courage and resolve to move through difficulties and setbacks?
- ✓ Do you, when it is practical, consult with those who will be impacted by a decision before it is implemented?

The main trait of **good leaders is being trustworthy.**
How is trust built and sustained? Here are the behaviors of what
trusted leaders do.   Now use these as a self-assessment. Do you
demonstrate:

- Integrity
- Honesty
- Fairness
- Loyalty
- Accountability
- Reliability
- Consistency
- Persistence
- Helpful
- Approachable
- Reachable
- Shares information

- Gives access
- Friendly & Kind
- Openness
- Caring
- Empathy
- Listens
- Takes others into account
- Dedication
- Engaged
- Competent
- Knowledgeable

Be an owner of your agency and of your performance
and take responsibility for building your professional reputation
with your every action. Your reputation is the most important
asset you have.   It is the summation of your performance,
character, experience, training, education, knowledge, skills and
abilities. After all, at the end of the day and at the end of your
career, after you have hung up the uniform and put aside the
formal authority that came with the position, your professional
reputation is all that you have. Your reputation will open doors
or limit your options. Do not give anyone the power to control
your reputation.

Here are ideas on how to plan and develop your professional skill set. Think of these as investing in your career development and, like in managing finances, you <u>must invest to earn any returns.</u>

Are you really serious about this? Or, do you just like <u>the idea</u> of being promoted?

If you have taken a promotional process before and did not succeed, what are you going to do differently? Remember the wise saying, "If you do what you have always done, you will get what you have always gotten." We said at the beginning that a shift of thinking is absolutely essential to be a supervisor. Have you really made that shift?

Here is a success story to consider: Frank had been with the Police Department for 10 years. He had spent most of his career in patrol and had worked traffic enforcement as a motorcycle officer for several years. When he took his first promotional test, he was president of the officer's labor guild. Looking back on this performance, Frank said that he did poorly because he thought and talked like a line officer and the union president. He did not see the whole picture, he did not support the department's leadership team, and he knew nothing about the broader issues of personnel, budget, public perceptions and helping employees to succeed.

What separated Frank from most candidates was his willingness to hear the honest criticism from successful supervisors and managers. He sought them out and took their advice. Most importantly, Frank made a commitment to re-invent himself, to break out of his comfort zone and to try new experiences. Frank did the work and shifted his thinking to being a supervisor. The results came at the next promotional test, two years later, and Frank was the top scoring candidate.

Think about these categories for self-evaluation and the more of them you do, the more prepared you may be for the next opportunity. Think of each of these as small steps to changing how you think and view supervision.

A. STUDY MATERIALS AND DOCUMENTS

✓ Study the job description for the position.

✓ Study these critical documents: strategic plan, budget, policy and procedure manual on high risk/low frequency events, and the annual report.

✓ Study the current collective bargaining agreement and the rules that govern working conditions.

✓ Study and embrace the agency's mission, vision, values and core principles.

B. INTERVIEW

✓ Talk to people who are in the position and learn what they do, how they do it, and why they do things a certain way. What are the current problems and issues?

✓ Ask senior managers what they are looking for in a top candidate and apply that learning. What are the emerging philosophy, programs, issues and priorities within the agency? What are the current and emerging labor-management issues? What is on the horizon and how can you prepare for it?

✓ Find out from community or elected leaders what the concerns, issues and priorities of the community are and how these relate to the agency. What are the themes and priorities of the local government, now and in the near-term? What are they looking for from the next generation of leaders?

C. EDUCATION, SKILLS AND LEARNING

✓ Read and study about:

- o Situational Leadership because this applies well to policing where you need to adjust your leadership style to the situation and to the development level of your officers or deputies,

- o Servant Leadership because this can increase trust and build better team relationships.

- o The book, "Lincoln on Leadership,"

- o The art of negotiation and getting to mutual agreement,

- o Emotional Intelligence and learn about how to increase your self-awareness and the impact you have on others,

- o President's Task Force on 21ˢᵗ Century Policing, and

- o How to develop teams and small groups such as the forming, storming, norming, performing theory,

✓ Learn to create and deliver a genuine feeling of care and understanding of people that is expressed with excellent listening skills and an emphasis on empathy and humility.

✓ Start the next level of formal academic course of study. For first level supervision, an associate's degree is essential; for management, a bachelor's degree is often needed.

✓ Commit to staying current to changes in case law and trends in policy and procedure.

✓ Be fluent in the agency's high risk and high liability policies and procedures and those that directly apply to the position being tested for.

✓ Be a journeyman user of MS Word, Excel & PowerPoint.

✓ Develop a college-level ability in writing.

✓ Develop and practice public speaking skills.

✓ Become oriented to budget, accounting, and fiscal planning topics because that is often where the real power of an agency lies.

✓ Be savvy and comfortable with the current information technology.

✓ Read at least two books on leadership every 6 months.

✓ Learn the skill of project management as this is used often in management and administration.

D. EXPERIENCES

✓ Be a positive influence within the agency by seeking ways to better and efficiently achieve the agency's mission and supporting the agency's leadership.

✓ Top candidates are well rounded and many have excelled in several different assignments.

✓ Volunteer to participate in planning a complex or important event or project.

✓ Find a coach who will guide you.

✓ Be a formal or informal spokesperson or representative of your agency.

✓ Be persistent about achieving your goals.

✓ Find a critic who will be honest with you about your writing and oral presentation skills, command presence and other aspects of your performance.

✓ Hone your thinking to view issues like a supervisor rather than a line employee. Visualize being in the position, listen to unfolding critical events and ask yourself, "What would I do?"

✓ Be involved in crafting a staff study or a proposal for your agency.

✓ Study and experience providing leadership in managing critical events.

✓ Coach and counsel co-workers and peers to help them improve.

✓ Learn from the success, setbacks, and lessons learned of others.

✓ Initiate a job-shadow experience with a respected manager and leader.

✓ Experience a promotional process by being a role player or an assessor if you are a supervisor.

E. TRAINING

✓ For supervision, complete at least one of the nationally recognized supervision courses: Northwestern University's School of Police Staff & Command, FBI National Academy, or the Southern Police Institute.

✓ For law enforcement management, complete the IACP course in Leadership of Police Organizations. In Illinois, pay attention to the courses offered by the Western Illinois University's Executive Institute.

✓ Attend professional conferences, even at your own expense.

✓ Read the current professional literature.

✓ Study national and regional reports to analyze trends and results.

✓ Learn how to better manage your time, prioritize tasks and be organized.

✓ Be a master at competently dealing with difficult people and resolving conflict.

✓ Develop the ability to accomplish work through and with other people and to see the ramifications of a course of action.

✓ Develop the ability to

  o Plan and manage a project,

- ○ Monitor a budget,

- ○ Evaluate employees,

- ○ Make budget projections,

- ○ Distinguish between wants and needs, and

- ○ How to accomplish the goals and objectives of the agency.

F. PERSONAL DEVELOPMENT

✓ Take self-assessment tools to learn your communication style, your personality and how to be effective with other people.

✓ Learn about and develop within yourself these characteristics: integrity, courage, emotional intelligence, vision, passion and judgment.

Key Theme: Your employer may provide opportunities and offer incentives or support, but if you wait for the employer to develop you, it is highly likely that you will be out-competed by the top candidates who are driving and investing in their career development.

THE VALUE OF A COACH

A coach is a knowledgeable guide who can give quality advice, teach, provide experiences, tell you the truth even when it is difficult, and believes in your potential. The value of having a coach cannot be overstated. From personal experience, after failing a promotional process, I was pointed to a coach who provided me the keys to success and how to prepare and this gave me the confidence to later be in the top tier of candidates.

Find a coach who will:

- Assess your strengths and weaknesses,
- Help devise a plan to mitigate your weaknesses,
- Share the reasons behind their success,
- Offer experiences that will prepare you,
- Provide honest and direct feedback,
- Point you to resources for self-improvement,
- Introduce you to other leaders whom you can learn from,
- Keep you on track, and
- Keep you focused on what is important and let go of what is not.

THE KEY THEMES IN REVIEW:

✓ Proper planning and preparation prevents a piss poor performance.

✓ Your attitude about the promotional process and being the new supervisor is one of the most important tools that you have.

✓ Be an owner of the best possible work performance.

✓ Take responsibility for building your professional reputation with your every action.

✓ Your employer may provide opportunities, may offer incentives or support, but if you wait for them to develop you, it is highly likely that you will be out-competed by the top candidates who are finding and driving their career development.

FINALLY

Nothing good was achieved **without enthusiasm** and this is the most important attribute that will separate you from the other candidates and move you through the difficult times. The journey you are on is not easy. If it were, everyone would do it. There are many candidates who will try for the promotion, some out of ego and feel that they deserve it, some out of peer pressure because others are doing it but there are only a few who will truly apply themselves and work at putting their calling to make a difference through the leading of others into action. These candidates will develop their personal skill set and have the passion to be the next supervisor or manager.

About the Authors

After having successful careers in policing and education, John and Laurie Gray worked for Public Safety Testing, Inc. and created and administered assessment centers and promotional processes for 8 years. They have worked with over 800 public safety candidates and hundreds of assessors. They created and administered 150 custom-made promotional processes for police departments, Sheriff's Offices, communication centers, corrections and fire departments for the positions of first level supervisors, mid-managers and command. Over 98% of the candidates have rated their experience with these processes as fair and representative. They trained people to become test providers and administrators.

They coach candidates who desired to be in positions of leadership in police organizations. Many of their clients have done very well in the promotional process.

John Gray served in the law enforcement profession for 32 years; half of his career was with city police departments and the other half was with Sheriff's Offices and the National Park Service. He was a supervisor and a manager for 16 years that included 12 years as a Police Chief for two cities in Western Washington.

He has written promotional tests, been an assessor many times and has taught the topic of selection and promotion for the Northwestern University's national command school, the "School of Police Staff and Command." He is on the faculty of Western Illinois University's Executive Institute. He taught criminal justice classes at a community college for 10 years. He attended the International Association of Chiefs of Police workshop on conducting assessment centers.

John Gray has a Master of Education degree from Western Washington University with a focus on adult education; a Bachelor's of Arts degree from San Diego State University, is a graduate of Northwestern University's School of Police Staff and Command, the Northwest Law Enforcement Executive Command College and FBI LEEDS program; the International Association of Police Chief's Leadership of Police Organizations; and holds an Executive Certificate from the Washington State Criminal Justice Training Commission.

He is a Life Member of the Washington Association of Sheriffs and

Police Chief. As the committee chair for Accreditation he led a team that expanded the program for agency accreditation.

He has written articles on leadership and management topics that were in Police Chief Magazine, the FBI Bulletin, Law & Order Magazine, and Public Manager Magazine. He is the author of a book, *The Boss's Interview; How to Separate the Job-Seeking Pretenders from the Contenders*. He co-authored the book, *Going the Distance, A Candidate's Guide to Promotional Testing and Assessment Centers* with Laurie Gray

Laurie Gray is a career educator with over 30 years of teaching experience. She earned a Bachelor's Degree from the University of Washington and was a certified teacher in Washington State. She has worked in a variety of educational settings including public schools, the National Park Service, a public utility, a beach ranger program, and a children's museum.

See their website for workshops and services:

www.jlgraycompany.com

Email: johnlgray425@icloud.com

Fun fact: As avid boaters, John and Laurie have published articles and created blogs with photos on their cruising experiences. They have cruised the Salish Sea, the Inside Passage and the Great Loop. They are full-time cruisers on Puget Sound. John is a licensed Captain, does on the water instruction and together, they present workshops to boaters.

See their boating websites:
www.tribute-kadeykrogen39.com
www.andiamo-ranger29.com
www.laurieann-ranger25.com

Made in the USA
San Bernardino, CA
25 July 2019